Language, Lies & Irrational Thinking

David Garnett

A Defence of Reason in an Unreasoning World

To the Julias in my life.

David Garnett

David is a retired university teacher and researcher. He lives in Monmouth with his wife Julia and their rescue dog Whipple. He has written extensively on policy and social justice and has acted as a consultant to a number of organisations in the UK and overseas. He has a wide experience of practical policy making and acted as chair of four voluntary bodies in the fields of disability, housing, and environmental protection. He recently retired (2016) as chairman of the board of Centigen FM Ltd. a rapidly expanding Facilities Management company. He is also currently acting as a strategic advisor to ND Metering Solutions, a manufacturing company based in Bradford with operating links around the world. He has contributed to the international literature on inter-generational justice. In retirement he maintains his interest in Philosophy, research and education.

He likes cricket and amuses himself by writing dreadful doggerel verse with obvious rhymes and dreadful puns.

An Investigation into Dysfunctional Discourse

“*David Garnett's masterly dissection of the notion of dysfunctional discourse should be read by anyone wishing to understand how contemporary policy discussions have become so toxic. In my view there is no other volume that deals with the issue of decision-making in a complex multi-agency environment with similar clarity and sophistication.*”

(**John Pitts** Vauxhall Professor of Socio-legal Studies at the University of Bedfordshire and Visiting Professor of Criminology at the University of Suffolk and the North China University of Politics & Law in Shanghai.)

Acknowledgements

I am indebted to those friends and colleagues who took the time to read the text in its various drafts and who offered many helpful suggestions. I owe particular debts of gratitude to Professors Fred Inglis and John Pitts. The former helped me focus the argument. The latter provided invaluable criticisms and helped edit the final draft. I am especially grateful to Peter Rennoldson for his patience and attention to detail in managing the publication process. I would also like to thank Heather Allan for her advice and support. Heartfelt thanks go to my wife Julia for the time she devoted to discussing the book's ideas as well as proof reading the text. I, of course, take full responsibility for any errors of scholarship.

This book is a Leaping Frog publication 2020 and is produced in conjunction with the Garnett Foundation. All proceeds will be donated to charity. Leaping Frog publications is a small independent publishing house.
Book design by Big Carrot Design

Illustrations** (unless stated otherwise) **by Peter Rennoldson

ISBN: 978-1-9997537-0-2

Table of Contents

Preface

"Everybody calls "clear" those ideas that have the same degree of confusion as his own." (Proust)

The premise of this book is simple enough, namely that the ways in which we talk to each other are resulting in irrational decisions and unsustainable policies. The book's central argument is that the quality of our decision-making would be improved if we spent more time and effort considering why people make the claims they do rather than simply reacting to such claims. In examining the 'whys and wherefores' of how people justify arguments the text examines the ways in which different, often competing, rationalities are expressed in policy debates. In many respects, the arguments presented can be treated as a series of essays about communication and miscommunication. Although much of the argument is inevitably (and unapologetically) grounded in theory, its intention is to provide a way of responding to a key practical issue – namely, how to make policy decisions that we do not live to regret.

By amplifying decision-making theory and practice the text offers a timely contribution to the more general debate about what counts as a 'rational decision'. It introduces and explores the idea of **Multiple Rationality Analysis** and makes concrete suggestions about how, in an age of mass information, the idea can be used to improve the quality of strategic thinking. Those trying to understand how to go about analysing multiple rationalities can be confused by the different languages and methodologies used by social scientists from different fields. What the present volume offers, uniquely, is an accessible introduction to how people justify their 'claims to truth'. It brings together work from a range of social science disciplines and applies the insights gained to the kinds of theoretical and practical situations confronting policy analysts and decision makers.

For many years I have researched the mechanics of policy formation and decision-making in government (both central and local) and in business (both commercial and social). My interest became intensified when I was asked to chair the City of Bristol's Option Appraisal Exercise (required by all authorities prior to a vote of tenants about whether or not the council should retain its council housing landlord function). My role was to act as an independent 'honest broker' mediating the various interests involved in the decision. Over a number of months I managed a series of internal and external discussions between individuals and groups including tenants and leaseholders, members from various political parties, trade unions, central government officials, local authority managers, pressure groups, professional advisors and the media. This was a complex exercise requiring the creation of some sort of consensus between people with a variety of interests, attitudes, agendas and issues. Subsequently my learning from this exercise started me thinking about the relationship between rationality and decision-making. This book is, in part, the outcome of those deliberations.

Complex decisions involve more than simply choosing between options. In this book I emphasise the crucial importance of understanding how options are generated in the first place and make the point that options are created in discourse rather than discovered by research.

David Garnett
Monmouth
2020

INTRODUCTION

"Nothing is more disgraceful than insincerity."
(Marcus Tullius Cicero)

In this book I put forward the argument that the reason we make so many bad choices and instigate so many flawed policies is more to do with irrational thinking and mal-communication than a lack of knowledge. Most important decisions have several objectives and more than one outcome. A prominent feature of many business decisions, and virtually all social policy decisions, is that they are the result of debates in which an array of proposals have been considered. To be worthy of consideration, any proposed course of action has to be regarded as being in some sense 'rational'. This book analyses the various ways in which proposals are rationalized and decisions justified.

Who we are plays a large part in determining what we say. When we engage in dialogue, discussion or debate we bring to the table not only our arguments, but also our own particular mixture of beliefs, prejudices, attitudes and opinions. When discussing policies, to give our contributions greater credence, we tend to downplay the intimate relationship between 'self and statement'. We have what some theorists term a 'psychological interest' in presenting our opinions as facts – or at least as reasonable, justifiable statements. In the following essays I explore why and how people justify their opinions and then tentatively propose ways in which competing rationalizations might be reconciled with a view to making policy decisions that stand the test of time.

In this introductory essay I set the scene by discussing the socio-political context within which individual decisions are made and particular policies formulated. It is written in the first person because, compared with the rest of the book, it is more of a personal commentary than a scholarly paper. I will later look in some detail at how critical social theory, linguistics, and the social sciences in general can give us some insights into why it is we make important decisions that we later live to regret. Each chapter focuses on an aspect of distorted communication and the book as a whole seeks to explain why and how we make bad (including really bad) decisions. Where representative democracy is the standard form of government, it makes sense that the electorate should be informed: indeed, electors should not only be informed but also be capable of analysing options rationally. As Bertrand Russell observed some seventy years ago, although the general aim of the democrat is to substitute government by general assent for government by force, this implies the existence of a voting population capable of seeing things as they are.[1] This book is in part a plea for an improvement in the quality of both public debate and corporate decision-making.

The book's general argument is based on the precept that in the world of social affairs claims to truth emerge from discourse. Given its central place in the argument, the first chapter addresses the question of what it is that constitutes a 'decision discourse'. Subsequent chapters consider the various ways in which a decision discourse can become distorted. In this context, a sustainable policy is quite simply thought of as 'one we do not live to regret'. The proposition is simple enough - When misinformation or irrational thinking distorts a decision discourse, we are unlikely to make sustainable decisions. The significance of this seemingly obvious point of view is gathering weight in the public debate about the future of western democracies and their institutions. This is in part due to the appalling quality of recent general election campaigns and the increasing use of referendums to make highly complex social, economic and constitutional changes that will have major consequences for both present and future generations. It is also in part a reaction to what some people regard as a new type of populism that, to a large extent, is being conveyed by rapidly developing social media.

People living in western democracies who read newspapers, listen to broadcast news, engage with social media or talk to friends about world events, will be aware that in recent times something significant has changed in the way current affairs get talked about. To be more precise, the language used to advocate or criticise political and social policies has become aggressive and less amenable

[1] Russell B, 'Ideas that have harmed mankind' in Unpopular Essays (1950), Allen and Unwin. Reprinted, London & New York: Routledge, p.160.

to rational debate. The atmosphere of intolerance that pervades much of the public discourse is now so noticeable that it has itself become a subject of discussion. In the academic world, political theorists, psychologists, historians and social commentators are pointing to the breakdown of established social solidarities and the emergence of angry and resentful individuals and groups who are questioning many aspects of the neoliberal western political order. This trend of intolerance is seen by many as an offshoot of populist politics and the exposure of long-standing polarized views about the management of social affairs. The point being that when society's politically polarized nature becomes more apparent, discursive distortions intensify – and in turn these distortions then further strengthen the polarized nature of public opinion.

This shift came as a surprise to some commentators who not so long ago embraced Francis Fukuyama's 'End of History?' thesis.[2] Fukuyama argued that following the collapse of the Soviet Union, liberal democracy, coupled with market capitalism, would gradually (but inevitably) become the standard form of government throughout the world. His famous proposition was that authoritarian governments would slowly be replaced by liberal-minded administrations grounded in tolerant democratic political cultures. In particular he pointed to the European example of balanced collaboration to justify his claim that some form of western-style rational democracy would (in time) become a transnational norm. Simply put, he assumed that an aspiring international middle class that has a stake in creating and maintaining accountable, representative and stable governments would harness the freedoms and prosperity generated in western economies. For many this 'end of history' argument always seemed naive and recent events in both Europe and the US have had the effect of crystallizing these reservations into full-blown doubts about its actuality. The current prevalence of anti-establishment attitudes throughout the western democracies can be said to have largely undermined Fukuyama's 1989 vision of the future.

[2] Famously expressed as a propositional essay in 1989 in the American magazine National Interest and later, more assertively, in book format that dropped the question mark from the title: The End of History and the Last Man in 1992.

Post Truth

While Fukuyama believed that the advent of liberal democracy would free oppressed peoples from the lies and duplicity of totalitarian regimes, he seemed strangely unaware of what was happening at the very heart of liberal democracies. The apparent shift towards a modern post-truth age did not begin, as some argue, with the election of Donald Trump. Indeed, in terms of presidential influence, the scene was set by Richard Nixon and Watergate and latterly by the words and works of George W. Bush. As it has been written up by commentators, one of the key moments in the post-truth narrative occurred when in 2004 a senior advisor to President Bush, later identified as Karl Rove, told the journalist Ron Suskind that the problem with people like him was that they lived in "the reality-based community" and what they failed to understand was that "we" (the Administration) now create our own reality. Perhaps inevitably, this widely reported encounter opened up a wave of criticism of what was interpreted as the Administration's scant concern for what is real and a desire to replace it with a more politically convenient reality based on fantasy.[3]

Of course, individuals and groups seeking to achieve advantages by misrepresenting reality have always distorted public discourses. Machiavelli himself was instructing princes in the art of grand deception in the early sixteenth century. His 1522 advice to Raffaello Girolarni prior to his appointment as an imperial ambassador has a contemporary ring about it:

> *"And if, to be sure, you sometimes need to conceal a fact with words, do it in such a way that it does not become known, or, if it does become known, that you have a ready and quick defence".[4]*

The apparent 'new moral order' is variously labelled "the post truth age", "post truth politics", "the age of anger", and "the age of cynicism". I would contend that it is not so much an "age" or coherent political system as a phenomenon. Much academic effort is currently being expended on explaining what socio-economic forces lie behind

[3] It should be said that the conversation as reported in the New York Time Magazine was denied by Rove and in fairness to the advisor, even if (as is probable) he did say what was reported, he might have been using a little irony to make the point that progress requires breaking free from the constraints of present realities and static opinion.

[4] Antony Jay (1996), Oxford Dictionary of Political Quotations, OUP.

this phenomenon. A trawl through this literature shows a wide range of assumed reasons for the attitudinal shift. A number of factors have been variously put forward to help explain what appears to be taking place. These include a general disillusionment with representative democracy by marginalized groups as a result of the widening disparity between rich and poor; the loss of identity that has accompanied the emergence of a global culture; the rise of secular fundamentalism; the increasing influence of social media and its preoccupation with conspiracy theories; the oversimplification of complex issues in social networks and the media; and a weakening of established forms of authority and legitimation. Together these forces have had the effect of replacing healthy scepticism with unwholesome cynicism.[5]

It is not only the poor, the weak and the disenfranchised who are disillusioned and becoming cynical. In the intellectual air, so to speak, there now exists an appreciation amongst those middle-class commentators (like myself) who think seriously about these things that all is not well with the state of social and political debate. Those of us who cannot claim to have been 'left behind' by the march of economic progress, have nevertheless become disillusioned about how public affairs are being conducted. This cynicism stems not simply from the inappropriateness of the policies being advocated by those with influence, but also by the ways in which those policies are being justified. It is this concern with the language of rationalization that is the focus of this little book of essays.

It is perhaps the universality of modern cynicism that distinguishes it from that operated in earlier times. The internet has a lot to answer for in this regard. It was developed with the specific intention to enhance our ability to communicate facts and information. More than anticipated, it has been a democratising force – which is no bad thing in itself. It has also helped to undermine deference by challenging established sources of authority - which again is not necessarily a bad thing. More significantly, and certainly more concerning, it has given a voice to some people with extreme or

[5] In a post-modern world in which everything is reduced to a text and 'the truth' is reduced to a plurality of competing 'truth claims', none of which has a necessary counterpart in the real world, many people feel that they are adrift in a sea of confusion and some are saying that the increasingly polarized nature of public debate means that they are becoming "politically homeless".

irrational views who in earlier times had little or no influence because they were scattered and isolated and unable to create an audible argument. Ideologues and conspiracy theorists can now use the internet to join forces with a variety of manipulating agencies to make a disturbing noise that is specifically designed to drown out rational argument.

The over-hanging question remains, 'Are things different now – are we really living in a post-truth world or are we simply living in a modern world in which it is deference that has been undermined rather than fundamental trust?' The underlying argument of this book is that things really are different now. The prevalence of 'fake news' and widely held irrational arguments in the public sphere is producing a discursive climate in which the traditional sources of reliable information are being undermined. The ubiquitous internet is now even providing a self-referencing falsehood feedback loop. It is not only contaminated with misinformation but it allows the distributors of phoney information to defend themselves with references that they have sourced from the very same unreliable internet. The universality of fake news and misinformation is beginning to create a discursive atmosphere where no-one is trusted. When no-one can be trusted, there is a tendency to turn to those sources with which we are most comfortable – that is, those that best reflect our preconceptions, interests and prejudices.

When, on 3 June 2016, Michael Gove, the then UK's Justice Secretary and leader of the campaign to leave Europe was challenged on Sky News by being presented with critical reports from the IMF, the Bank of England, the TUC, the CBI and a battery of leading economists, he famously replied that the British people "had had enough of experts". Although this comment opened up Gove to much ridicule, it is worthy of note that he was not the first British politician to demonstrate distrust in experts. In a letter to Lord Lytton dated 15 June 1877, Lord Salisbury commented that, "No lesson seems to be so deeply inculcated by the experience of life as that you never should trust experts."

(Quoted by Antony Jay (2001), Oxford Dictionary of Political Quotations, OUP)

'Fake news' used to have a limited and specific meaning. It was used to describe lies and misinformation that were deliberately planted in, and spread by, the media (particularly social networks). Since the 2017 US presidential election, the term has not only come into more prominence, but its meaning has also been widened to include facts that politicians and political campaigners do not like. In the febrile world of party politics, the term 'fake news' is increasingly being used to dismiss evidence that appears to undermine ideologically driven policy proposals and the term is now often used to dismiss a news report that is factually correct. The most insidious examples occur when a fact is challenged by a downright lie that is presented as "an alternative fact". A less insidious approach to this form of distorted policy discourse occurs when a small presentation error is made and this is then highlighted and used to claim that the whole report is "fake". [6]

Some would suggest that the emergence of an age in which objective facts are deemed to have less influence in shaping public opinion than appeals to emotion and personal belief can be dated with some precision. Increasingly, commentators are suggesting that its occurrence in western politics is subsequent to and to a large extent as a result of, fractious campaigns for the US presidency and Britain's withdrawal from the European Union. Donald Trump began his campaign by supporting a phoney claim that President Obama was born outside of the USA and that the use of an audio recording in his own (Trump's) voice describing how he used his celebrity to gain sexual gratification by groping women was "not true". 2016 also marks the oft-referred-to occasion when obvious misinformation about the positive financial consequences of Brexit were displayed on the side of a bus.

It is understandable that to many, the political world's moral axis seems to have recently tilted towards crass hypocrisy and cynicism. However, in his recent writings on the nature of 'truth',[7] the academic philosopher Simon Blackburn makes the point that the fact that Trump's lies have caused so much outrage should be seen as evidence of a wide concern that honesty in public life is still highly valued. Having said this, Blackburn does concede that something real has changed in public attitudes towards truthfulness. Although not measurable in any meaningful sense, it is

[6] This is a particular feature of climate change deniers' attacks on scientific evidence.

[7] Blackburn S (2005), Truth: A Guide for the Perplexed, London: Penguin Books. (ii) Blackburn S (2017), Truth: Ideas in Profile. London: Profile Books

clearly the case that we tend to moralise less about public dishonesty than used to be the case a generation ago. Although no one simplistic phrase fully captures the cultural changes that seem to be occurring, I am inclined to describe the current state of affairs as 'the age of political insincerity' rather than 'the post-truth age'. Although the pursuit of truth is still advanced as a fundamental societal value and delusion is seen as a dangerous trait, we do appear to have become more tolerant of hypocrisy in public and corporate life.

Delusion resides in the gap between fact and belief - hypocrisy in the gap between logic and personal interests. The deluded are dangerous but sincere. Hypocrites, on the other hand, are dangerous and insincere. When the deluded wield influence, the world can become a strange and dangerous place. Delusion insulates those in power from alternative ways of thinking and this is problematic when the deluded possess the power to influence important decisions. Like the poor, the deluded are always with us. Also, like the poor, outside of cults and sects, in western democracies at least, the deluded seldom wield much deep-seated, long-term influence. This is not the case with hypocrites. Within the broad community of the insincere, persistent hypocrites represent a particularly evil clan. They are not so much deluded as manipulative. The deluded can be dangerous but they cannot help themselves: not so the hypocrites. Hypocrisy is the way in which a knowingly distorted discourse is justified. When hypocrisy becomes strategic, truly malevolent forces are set in motion.

Innocent and expected hypocrisy

Of course, hypocrisy takes many forms – not all of which are malevolent. In many instances hypocrisy can be regarded as a mature social skill that we acquire as part of a broader package of social niceties. In everyday life, hypocrisy can be the glue that holds many of the little subtleties of social interaction together. In most decision meetings there will exist what might be termed 'expected hypocrisies'. These are verbal, written or physical acts of insincerity that are not only accepted but actually expected as part of the process of doing business in political and corporate life.

An insurmountable barrier to free and open discourse exists when duplicity masquerading as authenticity is accepted as normal. Decision discussions are inevitably affected by the ways in which people project themselves and both academic psychologists and populist tweeters and pamphleteers make much of the point that surface appearances such as dress and demeanour, carry weight in both public arenas and more intimate interpersonal settings. In his text The Presentation of Self in Everyday Life (1956), the American psychologist Erving Goffman, famously used the imagery of the theatre to describe human interaction. Since that date, the metaphor of a 'performance' is constantly used to describe the socio-psychological nature of both social and business relationships.

Until recently, these 'performance behaviours' have not been seen to be particularly problematic. We might draw an analogy here with the use of white lies in domestic or other informal settings. Familial and friendship relations can be enhanced by the use of innocent deceptions and business and political life eased by the employment of orchestrated interpersonal rituals that carry the force of expected good manners. Indeed, these expected good manners are often referred to as "professional behaviour". To dress comfortably or write your own speeches in public (particularly political) life can be seen as inappropriate and often invites strong criticism or even ridicule. As every diplomat knows, genuinely being oneself in public life is difficult and seldom recommended as a way of achieving sought-after outcomes.

A recent case that illustrates this point occurred in May 2016 when at a party in honour of the Queen's ninetieth birthday, David Cameron, the then British Prime Minister, made unguarded remarks to the monarch about the forthcoming anti-corruption conference he was about to chair. His remarks that the leaders of some "fantastically corrupt" countries - "Nigeria and Afghanistan" - will be attending were caught on camera and microphone. Despite the fact that his remarks reflected a generally accepted fact (already publicly conceded by the Presidents of both countries), Cameron was subsequently subjected to strong criticism from many quarters for failing to act "properly" – i.e. 'diplomatically'.

Malevolent hypocrisy: the Russians have a word for it

Our concern in this book is with a particular type of hypocrisy – or to be more precise, a particular set of hypocrites. We will call this malevolent set of dissemblers 'The Mumpsimus Mob'. A mumpsimus is defined as a stubborn person who insists on making an error in spite of being shown that it is wrong. Supposedly, this derogative term originated in Tudor times with a semi-literate priest who said "mumpsimus" instead of "sumpsimus" ('we have taken' in Latin) during mass. When his mistake was pointed out to him, the arrogant cleric rebuffed his critics and refused to substitute sumpsimus for his meaningless word mumpsimus.

In the above group of ne'er-do-wells we see a cross-section of more-or-less malevolent hypocrites. The notions of vranyo and lozh may not be familiar as they are terms derived from the cultural experiences of the Soviet Union. The terms have no exact parallels in English and they represent two similar forms of lying. Vranyo exists when speakers or writers know that they are not speaking the literal truth and they expect their audience to understand that this is the case. For vranyo-telling to exist there have to be listeners who pretend to believe what is being told. A vranyo lie involves a two-way collaboration.

When Donald Trump on the 2016 campaign trail gave a speech in Iowa in which he made the claim that he could stand in the middle of Fifth Avenue and shoot somebody dead without losing any votes, he was committing a sort of ironic vranyo. Both he and his audience knew that his claim would not literally be true but through their gestures[8] and applause, reacted as though it were so. A Russian friend of the correspondent of the New York Times David Shipler explained vranyo in this way: "You know I'm lying, and I know that you know, and you know that I know that you know, but I go ahead with a straight face, and you nod seriously and take notes."[9]

The day after his inauguration he falsely accused the media of lying about the size of the crowd attending this inauguration event (the numbers compared unfavourably with those attending the inauguration of President Obama). Although the row was over a seemingly trivial issue (comparative crowd sizes), it highlighted a concern that was to grow in significance throughout Trump's term in office. The crowd size argument was played out in the media and the lozh effect deepened when in an interview with NBC's Chuck Todd, Sean Spicer, the White House press secretary, defended the President's claim by arguing that he was merely presenting "alternative facts". Todd responded by saying that, "Alternative facts are not facts – they're falsehoods". Arguably, this interview marks the point at which lozh became a standard weapon in the armoury of White House propaganda.

One important way in which this phenomenon is different from what is normally understood by the term 'hypocrisy' is that it necessarily involves a degree of group participation that gives it a strong cultural dimension. Although Trump's claim regarding the imaginary Fifth Avenue incident was understood to be pure theatre, it does contain an important insight into contemporary American society: in certain circles, the attachment to truth has clearly become tenuous.

[8] Trump mimicked firing a gun.

[9] Shipler D (1983) Russia: Broken Idols, Solemn Dreams, pp.21-25.

Although not usually manipulative in a malicious sense, Vranyo can be morally reprehensible. When an employee or co-worker says they will complete a task in a certain time but has no intention of so doing and the line manager or colleague knows this to be the case but chooses not to confront or expose the lie – that would constitute vranyo. Both parties understand that the line manager (as part of her job) has to ask about the task timeframe and both parties know that the answer will not be true. There is no major manipulation going on – it is simply the way all concerned expect the usual ineffective management controls to operate in this particular organization.

Vranyo involves collusion between the speaker and the listener. The Trump example mentioned above illustrates this distinguishing feature. While vranyo is an exercise in imagination – a tall tale told to amuse or make a point, or play some sort of cynical management game – lozh implies a conscious intention to deceive. On the occasion of his pre-caucus speech in Iowa, some of his critics would say that – unusually - Donald Trump was not seeking to deceive his audience: he was commenting, correctly as it turned out, on the robustness of his core support. On this occasion, Trump was engaging in vranyo rather than lozh.

Lozh is a form of lying that is truly mendacious: its intention is to deceive and influence the opinions of others in order to gain some individual or sectional advantage. It is a form of barefaced lying that is not intended to be challenged. Trump's presidency soon became associated with lozh and this eventually led to calls for his impeachment. It began with a series of falsehoods, originated by Trump himself, that were designed to undermine the credibility of his critics in the media.[10] The argument advanced in these essays is that, along with a lack of self-awareness (see chapter 6), dishonesty distorts the discourse. We might say, with apologies to Lord Acton, that dishonesty distorts the discourse and fundamental dishonesty distorts it fundamentally. Of the various factors that distort the decision discourse, lozh represents the extreme case. The question is therefore, "How do

[10] The scene for this type of mendacious politics was set before Trump took office. In 2016, "post-truth" was chosen as the Oxford Dictionary's Word of the Year due to its prevalence in the context of that year's Brexit referendum and the media coverage of the US presidential election.

we deal with lozh in public life? Insincerity and gullibility are the two great allies of deception and authenticity is its greatest enemy. This general proposition is discussed in some detail in chapters 2 to 5. In chapter 7 the point is made that the two integral virtues of truth telling are sincerity and accuracy and chapter 8 makes the point that authenticity is about 'integrity' and 'true motive'.[11]

The relationship between power and hypocrisy is interesting and, given the positive correlation between power and influence, has real significance in the political decision-making process. A series of Dutch research projects in the early twenty-first century concluded that the idea of entitlement plays a crucial role in this relationship between power and influence and that it is only when power is experienced as legitimate that moral hypocrisy can come about. If the power is not regarded as legitimate then the "moral hypocrisy effect" does not take root. If this is true – and let us assume that it is – then we can argue that an effective weapon in the defence of reason in public life can be the systematic analysis of how those members of the Mumpsimus Mob who wield power and influence justify their arguments. Put simply, if we want to protect ourselves from lies and misinformation, we have to delegitimize the irrational arguments of the liars and dissemblers.[12] A key theme that permeates the book's overarching argument is that more attention should be given to how those with influence rationalize what they say.

Advertising and the distorted discourse

Malicious hypocrites are insincere and have no commitment to accuracy: the success of their mission to distort the discourse is dependent upon them being able to dominate the media in a way that prevents proper consideration of what counts as 'authentic'. Concerns about the role played by advertising in the creation of 'false news' have recently come to the fore. In October 2019, Twitter announced that it is to ban all political advertising worldwide,

[11] As long ago as 1790, the Irish political commentator Edmund Burke made the point that hypocrisy can afford to be magnificent in its promises because it never intends to fulfil them. (Reflections on the Revolution in France).

[12] When the powerful feel that their power is legitimate they are also likely to feel entitled to more leeway in their own actions and thoughts. As the Dutch researchers noted, "the powerful impose more normative restraints on other people, but believe that they themselves can act with less restraint." Lammers, J., Stapel, D.A. & Galinsky, A.D. (2010). Power Increases Hypocrisy: Moralizing in Reasoning, Immorality in Behavior. Psychological Science. DOI: 10.1177/0956797610368810.

arguing that the reach of such messages should be "earned" by attracting followers and not simply "bought" for cash. By contrast, Facebook, that makes millions of dollars of revenue from such ads,

has ruled out such a ban. It was in the late 1950s that Vance Packard famously explored how advertisers used motivational research and psychological techniques to influence patterns of consumption in the buoyant American post-war economy.[13] Packard's book also critically explored the manipulative techniques used by poli-

[13] Packard V. (1960), The Hidden Persuaders, London: Penguin Books.

ticians to influence people's voting preferences. During the 1960s the book and its message were highly influential: as well as being constantly discussed in and on the popular media, it featured as a standard text on a wide range of higher education reading lists – including those concerned with marketing, sociology, economics, psychology and teacher training. Although mass demand has been created almost entirely through commercial advertising, Packard almost certainly exaggerated advertising's power to deceive. Today many of his assumptions about the scientific manipulation of the consumers' psyche by advertisers are questioned and we no longer hear much serious debate about such techniques as subliminal messaging.

The advertising industry developed alongside the evolution of capitalism. Much commercial advertising can be classified as informational and has been regulated in a way that - until now – has allowed overtly false claims to be challenged in the courts. This was not always the case.

> *"First you make people believe they have a problem, and then you sell them the solution. That's how advertising works. Every snake oil salesman knows that." (Oliver Markus Malloy)*[14]

There is no guarantee that in the twenty-first century the law will be able to place adequate controls on what Shoshana Zuboff calls the "surveillance capitalists" who are already accumulating vast wealth and power in the ominous new "behavioural futures markets" where information about our attitudes and predictions about our behaviour are bought and sold.

Those of us in the western world born since World War II have grown up in a media-saturated environment and learnt a sort of advertising literacy that shields us from much of the crass psychological attempts to manipulate our behaviour. These days, we are as likely to be as sceptical of overstated product claims as we are to be persuaded by them. However, in some respects, it might be that our long association with the relatively innocuous culture of advertising has helped to acclimatise us to the idea that exaggerated claims and the spinning of information is normal and of no great

[14] *Bad Choices Make Good Stories – Finding Happiness in Los Angeles.*

importance. In other words, it might be the case that our long-acquaintance with commercial advertising has helped to 'soften us up' to the idea that political manipulation is to be expected and that it is of no great importance. In a digital age, this complacency might prove to be dangerous.

"Widespread intellectual and moral docility may be convenient for leaders in the short term, but it is suicidal for nations in the long term."
(Carl Sagan)[15]

Twitter's 2019 ban on all political advertising is of interest because it reflects a growing concern that digital technology is now facilitating a new form of exploitation of which we should all be concerned. The Facebook/Cambridge Analytica furore that be-

[15] Sagan C. (1999), Billions & Billions: Thoughts on Life and Death at the Brink of the Millennium. Cambridge: Headline Publishing Group.

gan to break in 2011, brought to the fore concerns that digital technology can now allow an individual internet user's personality to be easily and effectively predicted from public data and that such users "are dangerously unaware of the vulnerabilities that follow their innocent but voluminous personal disclosures".[16] Although the separate 'personality insights' themselves may be somewhat banal, their collection and subsequent sale to commercial and political agencies by such companies as Facebook, Snapchat, Microsoft and Google is producing a huge volume of information about consumers' and voters' attitudes and habits that is increasingly sophisticated and which has been harvested without their conscious consent. Future advertising will undoubtedly place an emphasis on the precision targeting of individuals and groups as a way of intensifying its effectiveness. Indeed, it is clear that in the United States, political campaigners are already using precision targeting in the belief that the acquisition of 'depth information' about individuals will enhance their ability to manipulate a populist culture and more effectively influence public opinion.

Populism

The use of the word 'populism' can be confusing. Unlike other '-isms' such as communism and fascism, populism is not an ideology or a movement but a way of communicating. It is a communication style that can be adopted by those on the left or the right, by liberals or conservatives – indeed by anyone putting forward a proposed programme of social reform. In the context of our discussion, 'popular' is a descriptive term and in making our argument, it is more useful to employ the adjective 'populist' rather than the noun 'populism'. In its adjectival form it more clearly carries pejorative undertones. When we describe a set of propositions as being 'populist' we mean our comments to be taken to be critical.

The key problem with populist politics is that it panders to those who want clear and simple answers to difficult problems, and this makes it more difficult to pursue intelligent policies that do justice to the complexity of the world. This is an issue that has to be addressed if we care about Enlightenment values (see chapter 4). It might be argued that through a process of enculturation some in-

[16] Zuboff S. (2019), The Age of Surveillance Capitalism, London: Profile Books, p.274.

dividuals can become partially immune from societal pressures to speak the truth (see chapter 6). It is not possible to get through life without, at times, being hypocritical; however, when hypocrisy becomes a character trait, we move from the normal and acceptable to the unreasonable and abhorrent. Habitual liars inhabit a world in which obsessive self-interest obliterates any sense of decency. In this condition, the person's mode of thinking becomes perversely distorted in ways that cause an automatic reflex to negate all aspects of reality that he or she finds disagreeable or in some other way objectionable. If the person proposing a falsehood believes it to be true in some way, then we are not so much dealing with hypocrisy as with ignorance. It may sound like a polemical point, but we really should be concerned about the voice of infantile populist politics, amplified by social media, allowing the ignorant and the mendacious to claim equality with the well-informed and the well-intentioned. It is not enough to 'speak truth unto power' - we also have to 'speak truth unto ignorance'.

It may well be that the rapid development of open access social networking has facilitated the spread of extreme populist ideas and that this democratisation of the ways in which opinions are dispersed has exposed a previously obscured fault-line in society: a line that used to inhibit the broadcasting of ignorant, reactionary and intolerant voices. Those whose opinions are tinged with (sometimes understandable) anger about how society has failed to recognise their concerns are more interested in airing their anger than debating issues.

The apparent weakening attachment to honesty might be regarded as a sort of distorted pragmatism (see chapter 4). What is occurring is arguably a belief by some that if it takes a lie to get a desired change – so be it. This notion of the ends justifying the means is, of course, a slippery slope. If we have to accept it as an unfortunate way of doing things in the modern world, we at least need to be fully aware of what is going on. Without such awareness, we would be in danger of losing not only our integrity, but also our grip on reality. If liars and language manipulators are now more readily forgiven, we nevertheless still have to recognise their falsehoods for what they are. A failure to do so would mean that such people have not simply distorted a discourse but undermined the very moral fabric of society. This has an obvious relevance to our current discussion. An awareness of falsehood and its potentially malign influence has to be maintained if we wish to develop social policies that we do not live to regret.

The motivation for writing these essays was essentially practical: that is, to ensure that our social policy decisions are 'warranted'. Because justifications that are illogical or intrinsically immoral result in outcomes we will live to regret, the subject matter of the book should be treated as an aspect of moral philosophy. This is because to count as 'warranted', as well as being a legal, effective and efficient, a social decision has to be ethical.

We go through life distorting the truth in order to make the stories we tell add up. Understanding why we mislead ourselves takes us into the field of psychology. Understanding why we make misleading statements to others catapults us into the realm of moral philosophy. By focusing on the big, overarching questions about the purposes of life and the nature of virtue, moral philosophy challenges the reasoning behind the statements we proclaim and the choices we make. Over the years philosophers have laid down normative rules of behaviour for determining how best to act in morally ambiguous situations. Ethics, the practical offspring of moral philosophy, addresses specific issues and dilemmas of moral concern and wrestles with the myriad of moral challenges that people face. These can range from momentous and highly personal issues such as whether to turn off the life support system of a loved one who is in a vegetative state to more general and minor concerns about whether it can be justified to lie to friends in order to make them feel better about themselves. Between these two poles of life and death decisions on the one hand and being polite to friends on the other, there exist innumerable ethical questions regarding our personal behaviour - typified by such questions as whether tax avoidance is always wrong or giving money to street beggars is doing 'good' or doing 'harm', and so on....and so on....

Although many (maybe most) of the decisions we make on a daily basis are driven by judgements that have at their base some form of moral imperative, this is not normally a matter of general concern because the vast majority of our decisions are inconsequential.

However, when we make a decision that will have a significant impact on our own life or the lives of others the reasons for making that decision should be understood and fully thought through. The need to understand how arguments are rationalized becomes particularly important if a proposed course of action is controversial, difficult to reverse, uses a large quantity of scarce and valuable resources, will have large-scale, long-lasting or wide-ranging consequences for vulnerable groups, will alter the natural environment, or affect the interests of future generations. Put simply, decisions that have ethical consequences require some form of moral justification.

The first and most important part of moral philosophy concerns the articulation of values (e.g. "people should not misrepresent the truth"). The second part concerns reasons (e.g. "these are the reasons why people should not misrepresent the truth"). The third part critically examines the validity of these reasons. It is this third element that provides the logical analysis upon which the other two rest - and it is this third aspect of moral philosophy that provides the focus of this book. Put succinctly, we will argue that to prevent making 'bad' decisions, we need to interrogate the justification not the claim.

In examining the 'whys and wherefores' of people's justifying arguments we will examine the ways in which different, often competing, rationalities are expressed in policy debates. This focus requires us to give a good deal of consideration to how language is used in defining and classifying values, ideas and events during the process of making decisions. In many respects, the arguments presented in the following chapters can be treated as a sequence of essays about communication and miscommunication. Although much of the argument is inevitably (and unapologetically) grounded in theory, its intention is to provide a way of responding to practical issues.

Sound decision procedures seek to establish deliberations that are rooted in a commitment to optimise outcomes that stand the test of time. The modest hope is that those applying the principles of what I am calling multiple rationality analysis (see chapters 1-4 and 8) will make better decisions than they otherwise would, had they not taken this approach to strategic thinking and planning. In what follows, as well as outlining the principles of multiple rationality analysis, I explore how traditional social science disciplines can help to disentangle logical thinking from the mesh of agendas, interests and values associated with the rationalisation of policy arguments. I examine how, in social affairs, claims to truth tend to be relative to the ways in which people think and talk about problems (what we understand to be the case) rather than any absolute 'truth' (what is the case). The book's initial chapters draw on ideas taken from philosophy, linguistics, psychology and anthropology and uses them to show how policy discourses can, and do, become distorted in ways that inhibit the open discussion of issues. In the later chapters it considers how the notion of multiple rationality analysis can be incorporated into the processes of strategic thinking about political and business policies – and as a result, make it less likely that we make decisions that we live to regret.

The Nature and Scope of Discourse

"At the end of reasons comes persuasion."
(Ludwig Wittgenstein)

Abraham Lincoln once asked, "If you call a tail a leg, how many legs does a dog have?" The answer, he said, is "four" because renaming doesn't alter truth. This anecdote tells us more about how language was regarded in Lincoln's time than it does about the nature of truth. It demonstrates what might now be regarded as an uncritical acceptance of the transparent nature of language and the power of established classifications. Nineteenth and twentieth century developments in semiotics and linguistics have brought to the fore important questions about the relationship between language and meaning. The modern philosopher might well challenge Lincoln's apparent conclusion that reclassification does not alter the 'truth' as expressed in discourse. Put simply, when we reclassify, we change our assertions about the nature of things. Indeed, in his own time, Lincoln himself believed that his legislative changes had real meaning and certainly did not accept the argument of Confederate slave owners that "you can amend the words of the Constitution but a slave is still a slave".[17]

In practice, policies are made in the context of some form of wider social interaction that we are here terming a mega-discourse. A mega-discourse embraces the whole complex of social interactions that operate to produce some sort of agreed understanding about the nature and scope of an area of social, commercial or political concern. In this way, it can be said that amongst an identifiable group of people living and working in a particular place at a particular time, there emerges a variety of 'mega-discourses' on such policy topic areas as transport, education, law reform, immigration, global warming, taxation, social care, and so on. Most local decisions are discussed within the cultural confines

[17] The sociologist W I Thomas (1927) said that when a situation is defined as real, it is real in its consequences.

of a mega-discourse. Although in this conception, dialogue is seen as an aspect of discourse, the term 'discourse' is being used here to describe a wider social phenomenon than that of a conversation between individuals. It is proposed that meanings are not only inscribed in spoken and written language, but that anything that signifies a point of view is considered to be part of the discourse. Although the old saying "actions speak louder than words" is, like so many aphorisms, folksy and simplistic,[18] it does, also like so many aphorisms, contain a recognisable element of truth. Much of what is eventually decided in decision meetings will be influenced by the background mega-discourse (that embraces spoken words, written texts, actions and symbols) in which such meetings are embedded. This over-arching discourse constitutes the socio-political context in which specific local decision meetings ('language events') take place. In our discussions we will consider the dynamics and mechanics of the discursive interactions between these two levels of discourse. This will involve drawing on ideas taken from both the so-called 'hard sciences' (particularly biology and neurology) and the so-called 'soft sciences' (philosophy, linguistics, psychology, anthropology, sociology and politics).

cognition and communication

This subject is so interdisciplinary that it is difficult to know where to begin. But begin we must: let us start with a statement that has profound implications and with which most people would agree.

Although neurologically speaking, we all think in the same way, social scientifically speaking, we do not all think the same thoughts.

If true, and let us assume that it is, this statement points to interesting questions concerning the relationship between cognition and communication that are of real current concern to all of the disciplines mentioned above. We will explore a number of these as our argument unfolds. Because our overall concern is with the communication of values and attitudes, we will begin by considering how meanings are, or are not, communicated through discourse.

[18] See chapter 2 and discussion of common sense wisdom.

Discourse and perception

"The President in Washington sends word that he wishes to buy our land. But how can you buy or sell the sky? The land? The idea is strange to us. If we do not own the freshness of the air and the sparkle of the water, how can we buy them?.....the Earth does not belong to man, man belongs to the Earth. All things are connected like the blood that unites us all. Man did not weave the web of life, he is merely a strand in it. Whatever he does to the web, he does to himself.....as we are part of the land, this Earth is precious to us."
(Chief Seattle 1852)

Chief Seattle was an ancestral leader of the combined Duwamish and Suquamish tribes. His now famous letter was written in reply to the United States Government's request to purchase Native American territory in the Northwest in 1852. The US government had already opened up tribal areas for settlers by allowing non-native Americans to claim Indian lands under the Donation Land Claim Act of 1850. During the 1850s commercial interests lobbied the federal administration to free more land of native title to allow for the construction of a transcontinental railroad. In 1855 the tribe was pressured into signing the Treaty of Point Elliott requiring it to relinquish rights over the remaining Suquamish territories.

Within his lifetime, the Chief had witnessed the transformation of his people's traditional ways of life into one dominated by settler values and attitudes. The Suquamish had to adapt their ancient culture based on fishing, hunter-gathering and travelling by river to accept a new economy and lifestyle forced upon them by foreign commercial, religious, social and political institutions. Missionaries, fur-traders and finally, permanent settlers brought new technologies, a currency system, alien legal arrangements, disease, and the concept of private property into their ways of living. These dramatic changes were more than physical and institutional: they were embedded in different ways of thinking and talking. The new imposed culture was not simply at odds with their established aboriginal traditions - it represented an alien value system that might be described as a different 'form of life'. Chief Seattle found that it was impossible to negotiate with authorities that did not share the values of his tribe's form of life. The two parties saw the world in such different ways that a meaningful discourse was impossible.

Contemporary notions of 'discourse'

Wittgenstein famously, but not always clearly, used the notion of 'form of life' to emphasise his belief in the underlying importance of a shared view of the cultural context within which discursive practices take place. He saw a form of life as constituting the necessary agreement in judgement that makes it possible for people to share ideas and communicate in a meaningful way. [19]

> *"If language is to be a means of communication there must be agreement not only in definition but also (queer as this may sound) in judgments."* [20]

Put simply, language depends for intelligibility on a common frame of reference. The gulf in understanding between white settlers and Native Americans in the eighteenth and nineteenth centuries went beyond disagreement about the definition of 'land' and 'ownership': it embraced fundamental judgements about the relationship between 'Man' and 'the Earth'. Wittgenstein's notion of forms of life is linked to his view of the nature of concepts, so that we might say that if an eighteenth or nineteenth century North American native says that it is not possible to own a tract of land and a European settler says that it is possible to own a tract of land, the disagreement does not reflect a simple difference of opinion about the definitions of words but a fundamental difference in judgement about the concept of 'ownership' which in turn relates to differing views about Man's relationship with the Earth itself.

Clearly, significant arguments about values and meanings can and do occur even within the context of what can be thought of as a

[19] Philosophical Investigations, translated by G.E.M. Anscombe , Oxford: Blackwell, (1968), remark. 226, p.88.
[20] Ibid. Remark 242, p.88.

common conceptual paradigm: vegan animal welfare campaigners can disagree with non-vegan animal welfare campaigners about the moral efficacy of consuming dairy products. It is clearly possible for people who broadly agree with each other on a range of issues to have specific and important points of view that are not held in common. It is partly for this reason that in our discussions we will regard Wittgenstein's notion of 'forms of life' as having only a limited use as an analytical tool and instead we will turn to contemporary notions of discourse that are more in sympathy with our argument's way of viewing the world (i.e. our hermeneutic stance). We will turn to a body of thought usually referred to as 'critical social theory' as a way of opening the door to a more convincing form of analysis that will help us to provide a more compelling explanation of the sources of discursive malfunctioning.[21]

A number of discretely different philosophical traditions have influenced current thinking about the nature and scope of 'discourse'. Arguably the most significant has been the post-Nietzschean European tradition associated with such names as Heidegger, Sartre, Gadamer, Derrida and Foucault that provided us with various ways of thinking about the nature of language and communication that emerged out of the Critical Theory of the 1930s and subsequent debates about structuralism and power relations. It has also absorbed and built on the ideas of what might be termed language theorists such as Saussure, Wittgenstein, Habermas, Austin, Searle, and Bernstein. In addition, we can say that the post-Darwinian Anglo-American tradition associated with such names as James, Dewey, Kuhn, Davidson, Rorty and Dennett have introduced a strong pragmatic perspective to the debate about what constitutes the essential nature of discourse: this latter group have done this by emphasising the part that self-interest plays in discursive interactions.

[Clearly other writers were influential in determining our current notions of 'discourse' and those mentioned here could be classified in other ways – Basil Bernstein, for example, always insisted that he was a sociologist rather than a linguist and Daniel Dennett describes himself as a cognitive scientist. This paragraph is simply intended to underline the fact that a variety of ideas lie behind the contemporary notion of 'discourse'.]

[21] *This approach will, for example, allow us to use notions such as 'ideal speech', 'speech communities', 'mutual knowledge', and 'cognitive dissonance' in our attempt to shed light on the nature and scope of dysfunctional discourse and its role in creating hypocritical statements.*

In everyday popular parlance, 'discourse' is taken to mean dialogue. Modern social scientists on the other hand have come to use the notion to describe sets of interrelationships that are more complex, subtle and important than simple 'talk'. Although dialogue remains the primary condition of this contemporary idea of discourse, the notion now also incorporates (some would say synthesises) a wide range of other observed social activities that have been highlighted by the academic thinking that has taken place over the last one hundred years. This has expanded the idea of discourse analysis from its original focus on textual interpretation and the scrutinising of what speakers do in conversation, to embrace anything that has an impact on how communication takes place in both personal and institutional settings.

Discourse is more than words

These days communication theorists make the point that discursive practices embrace more than written and spoken communication. In the social sciences it is now generally accepted that activities other than writing and talking can signify and thereby communicate meanings to those who participate in the interaction.

The old saying "a picture speaks a thousand words" is one of those trite aphorisms that contains a recognisable element of truth. [22]When in the late evening of September 31st 1938, the British Prime Minister, Neville Chamberlain, returning from his highly publicised trip to Munich to discuss the Czechoslovakian crisis with Hitler stepped off his plane onto the tarmac of Heston airport, he was "given one of the greatest ovations ever accorded to a British statesman".[23] Famously waving a piece of paper signed by himself and the German Führer, he triumphantly declared that the document was "symbolic of the desire of our two peoples never to go to war with one another again". In words that would soon return to haunt him, he declared: "My good friends, for the second time in our history, a British Prime Minister has returned from Germany bringing peace with honour. I believe it is 'peace for our time'".

The Munich Agreement has come to symbolize both the duplic-

[22] See chapter 2 and discussion of common sense wisdom.
[23] The Observer, 1 October 1938.

We, the German Führer and Chancellor and the British Prime Minister, have had a further meeting today and are agreed in recognising that the question of Anglo-German relations is of the first importance for the two countries and for Europe.

We regard the agreement signed last night and the Anglo-German Naval Agreement as symbolic of the desire of our two peoples never to go to war with one another again.

We are resolved that the method of consultation shall be the method adopted to deal with any other questions that may concern our two countries, and we are determined to continue our efforts to remove possible sources of difference and thus to contribute to assure the peace of Europe.

A Hitler

Neville Chamberlain

September 30, 1938

ity of the Nazi regime and the naivety of Chamberlain and the so-called 'appeasers' in his Cabinet. Subsequent to the Second World War, this event came to represent a significant moment that led to Chamberlain being replaced by Churchill and the emergence of a new realistic approach to Britain's relationship with Germany. Journalists, historians, teachers, and much of the public soon came to regard (interpret) the event as a turning point in British and world history. Historical meaning was, so to speak, read into the event at the airport. Arguably, Chamberlain's spoken words and his waving of 'the piece of paper' have become more recognizable as symbols of that change than the ostensible paper document itself.

Also arguably, nowadays, for most of us, the Nazi flag now imparts stronger feelings of hatred and revulsion than Hitler's words printed in Mein Kampf (that few have read). This is despite the fact that, at different times, in different cultures (including North American Indian tribes), the swastika symbol represented positive, life-giving values. The word "swastika" is derived from the Sanskrit "svastika" which refers to "well-being" and "good luck".

In modern discourse analysis the assumption is made that hermeneutics, which initially developed as the systematic interpretation of written texts, can be extended to embrace the study of human actions. This proposition is based on the ideas of writers such as Paul Ricoeur and Anthony Giddens who have argued that the human sciences can be said to be hermeneutical in as much as their objects of study display some of the features of actualised texts. If the meaning of a symbolic action can be objectified in a way that resembles a text then the methodologies for investigating such meanings can follow similar procedures to those of text-interpretation. This argument hinges on the proposition that human actions can have objectified meanings that are detached from the original event and continue to have a symbolic existence through time and space - depositing, so to speak, a 'trace' in history and carrying an imprint into the future that can subsequently be examined and analysed.

If we consider this argument through the eyes of linguistics and social theory, we might argue that what people write, say or do has significance: it carries an order of meaning. This significance can be ephemeral and restricted to a specific time and place - or be open and autonomous and be of more than a passing local interest: it can of course be both. In Basil Bernstein's work a crucial distinction is made between 'particularistic' and 'universalistic' orders of meaning.[24] These in some ways mirror Michel Foucault's distinction between 'discourse' and 'discursive formation'.[25]

'Peace In Our Time' Source: Ruben Oppenheimer, originally published in De Limburger newspaper November 2018.

A narrowly conceived 'discourse' assumes a dialogue articulated by the use of pronouns: its focus of meaning is local, immediate and particularistic. A discursive formation on the other hand, is authorless and operates in a wider field of universal meanings.[26]

[24] Bernstein B (1971), Class, Codes and Control. London: Routledge & Kegan Paul. To be absolutely clear, although Bernstein was often referred to as a linguist, he always insisted that he was a sociologist.

[25] Discussed below.

[26] Universalistic discourse employs meta-languages of public forms of thought with respect to both objects (as in the language of science subjects) and to people (as in the language of social science and arts subjects) so as to realize meanings of a universalistic nature.

Where orders of meaning are universalistic, the meanings are not tied to any time-specific given context of local relationships or a local social structure. When first published, the pictures of Chamberlain waving his 'piece of paper' constituted a particularistic (current and localised) news item. Over time, both the incident and its associated photographs have come to symbolise universalistic notions such as political naivety, bad faith, and the appeasement of tyrants and bombastic leaders.

The extended notion of discourse regards some human activity as being autonomous - that is, detached from the acting agent – analogous to Roland Barthes's idea that a text can be detached from its author. Where a text or an action takes on an independent identity, it can have consequences that are not part of a writer's (or speaker's / or actor's) original (local) intentions: indeed, it may carry potential meanings that simply were not conceived of by its originator. Others may appropriate aspects of a current discursive event sometime in the future as part of a different discourse. Jesus famously appropriated and repositioned the Hebrew legal dictum "an eye for an eye and a tooth for a tooth" (meaning a fair and just settled resolution to a dispute) to insist that punishments should be moderate and proportionate rather than retributory and equivalent (Matthew 5:38). These days the saying is used both by those advocating appropriately tough justice and those appealing for moderation. Hans Christian Anderson's story of the little boy exposing the delusions of an undressed emperor was (presumably) intended to be a moral tale by the author pointing out how difficult it is to 'speak truth unto delusional power'. Today this famous tale is still often referred to by critics of people who are assumed to be deluded in a similar way to that of the fictional emperor. However, because, like most folk tales, it can be appropriated and repositioned, it is also referred to by those claiming that a particular statement, policy or idea is knowingly false: that is, not so much delusional as straightforwardly dishonest. On a daily basis, quotations from the Bible, the Koran, Shakespeare, Abraham Lincoln, the film Star Wars, etc., are constantly taken out of their original contexts and used to illustrate, advance or challenge contemporary arguments.

By lifting (appropriating) a discursive event from its original context, clearly some of what it was or alluded to is annulled. Chamberlain certainly did not envisage his performance at Heston Airport being used by historians to represent British government naivety. And indeed, it was not at the time regarded as anything other than a reasonable (and welcomed) act of diplomacy – it is only in retrospect that it has widely been judged to be 'naïve'. Where discourse (including human action) is actualised as a sort of 'text' it displays non-ostensive references that go beyond the relevance to its initial spoken, written or acted situation. All of this means that it can be an 'open work' in the sense that, like a text, it can be addressed to a wide range of contemporary and future 'readers' who are then capable of drawing a variety of interpretations from it. The 'here and now' statements we make can be appropriated by others and repositioned (used in some later discourse) to create meanings we did not intend. In this way, a local (particularistic) discourse might be transposed, recontexualized and reactivated in order to achieve new meanings and different purposes.

Social meaning emerges out of engagement. Discursive engagement does, by definition, involve both a broadcaster and a receiver of statements - and meanings emerge from the interaction that occurs between the two. What I understand you to have said depends on what I take it to mean. The broadcast and the reception (the engagement) can be separated in time and place allowing for the possibility for a discourse to be free from the constraints that are attached to a specific, local, conversation.[27]

We can argue that where a discursive event (a human utterance or action) can be objectified and displays the characteristics of an autonomous 'text', it can be analysed not only by journalists and historians but also by those seeking to theorise about its nature and significance: it becomes available for analysis. This does not mean that all statements and actions have these analysable characteristics nor does it mean that those that do should be analysed; after all, most of what we say and do as we go through life is both transient and ephemeral and has little or no subsequent signifi-

[27] Bernstein B. 'Social class, language and socialization', in Abramson S A. et al (eds) Current Trends in Linguistics 12, Amsterdam: Mouton, 1971. pp.175-6. Referred to by Atkinson (1985) p.76.

cance even to ourselves. The point to be made, however, is that all actions may have these characteristics and thereby they have a potential to be transposed and recontexualized and as such, they have the potential to hold a lasting significance. Although this way of thinking stems from linguistics, its deeper roots are elsewhere – namely in Critical Theory and its more recent offspring 'critical social theory'.

Analysing discourse through critical social theory (CST)

Given its significance to the way in which we will build our argument, we need to lay down a clear and unambiguous definition of 'critical social theory'. In particular, we need to distinguish the notion from that of the 'Critical Theory' that is associated with the Frankfurt School of writers.[28]

> *Critical social theory (CST) is a philosophical approach to critiquing a society. It does this by applying knowledge from the social sciences and humanities with a view to exposing ideological constraints that prevent a proper understanding of social systems, structures of power, and other cultural factors inhibiting the emancipation of thought.*

Expressed in this way – particularly by using the notion of 'emancipation' - indicates CST's heritage in neo-Marxist thought and the ideas of the Frankfurt School of theoreticians. However, the philosophical foundations of modern critical social theory draw upon a wider range of influences than inter-war German idealism. Despite its intellectual heritage in established Critical Theory, critical social theory is used in ways that are not rigidly tied to the underlying assumptions of the Frankfurt writers of the 1930s. These earlier thinkers[29] were more overtly political and they drew on the psycho-social methodology of Freud as well as the historical analysis of Marx. The post-1970s critical social theory has inherited two important assumptions from the post-Freudian Frankfurt writers of the previous generation. The first was an understanding of power as a social relationship. The second was that meaning is tied to context.

[28] It is the convention to use upper case letters when referring to Critical Theory and lower case letters when referring to the more recent literature on critical social theory.

[29] Notably Herbert Marcuse, Theaodor Adorno, Max Horkheimer, Walter Benjamin and Eric Fromm.

The problem of analysis

Discourse analysis as a method of social scientific investigation was initially developed to analyse the structure of speaking and writing with a view to giving an account of the relationship of language to ideology. Discourse analysis, narrowly conceived, takes as its subject the language of everyday life. That is, it analyses the sentence sequences and structures in everyday texts and conversational exchanges as they occur in such places as newspapers, magazines, television programmes, classrooms, factories, offices and domestic homes. The usual sociological objective is to show how these patterns reflect relations of power. In short and simply put, it aims to uncover ideological implications in the apparently innocent structure of sentences.

Within the traditional, narrowly linguistic view of discourse, emphasis is placed on specific acts of communication. As such, context specific speaking (parole), unlike context free language (langue) has an identifiable subject in the sense of 'someone speaking' or 'someone writing'. This means that any spoken or written discourse (thus conceived) tends to employ pronouns to articulate relations between itself and others. Paul Ricoeur summarised this characteristic by saying that the "instance of discourse" is self-referential. (Ricouer (1981), Hermeneutics and the Human Sciences. Cambridge: CUP, p.198.) By using the phrase 'the instance of discourse', Ricoeur emphasised the temporal nature of the local discourse: and it is in this local, time-specific, sense that a discourse can be said to have an author. When an action signifies something, it can be treated as a discursive event and can be subjected to analysis in a similar way to that of a text or an utterance. In this sense, actions can be said to have an author whose intentions can be commented upon. Furthermore, if the action displays features that have a significance that extends beyond the initial incidence of the act and the intentions of the actor, it can be analysed as an autonomous occurrence ('authorless text') with a potential to contribute to future discursive events and involving altogether different human agents. To put it another way, what we do or say at a particular moment in a particular place has the potential to be reproduced and re-contextualised at some other time in some other place by someone else.

Extending the conception of discourse beyond speech and writing to embrace actions and images clearly brings into question the relevance of the analogy with 'authorship'. Can an action really be thought of as having some kind of 'author'? Some language events and actions are ephemeral and simply 'come and go' - having little or no long-term significance over and above what the 'author' intended in that moment and at that place. Others, however, are re-contextualised (we might say 're-authored') and thereby have a significance that extends beyond the time and place of their initial occurrence. In this way, a method of interpretation opens up that allows for a more universal, authorless meaning to be unshackled from the specific, initial, local occurrence of the (author-bound) dialogue. A documentary maker could incorporate a film clip of Chamberlain waving his famous piece of paper in order to illustrate a programme on the Life of Churchill. The documentary programme might then be shown to a group of students by a teacher to illustrate a lecture on 'The Causes of the Second World War'. A modern cartoonist might utilise the image in making a contemporary critique of what he sees as the appeasement of despots and autocrats. Also, of course, a writer might use the original incident and/or the contemporary cartoon to help build an argument about the nature and scope of discourse analysis....

Knowledgeability and Social Reproduction

Our ability to engage with discourse in ways that reproduce and develop social and institutional structures (agreed ways of doing things) is made possible by what psychologists refer to as our "practical consciousness". Anthony Giddens's elaborated the idea of practical consciousness to suggest that when we engage in dialogue we instinctively know what is going on. We have the potential to be aware (although not always in ways that we could describe) of the discursive 'games' being played and we have some sort of instinctive understanding of other people's hidden attitudes and agendas. This is a level of inherent understanding that is seated beneath our surface level of 'discursive consciousness' and of which normally we are not fully aware. In this way Giddens proposes that when we engage in dialogue with others we are, in a very particular sense, "knowledgeable actors".

Giddens's structuration theory seeks to explain how this deep-seated knowledgeability of actors is implicated in the progressive reproduction of society's ideas and institutions. The theory suggests that human agency and social structures are interrelated (exist as a duality). More specifically, structuration theory seeks to shed light on the dynamics of institutional change and

> *"Agents can sometimes express their reasons for what they do in verbal or discursive form.....But this by no means exhausts what they know about why they act as they do. Many most subtle and dazzlingly intricate forms of knowledge are embedded in, and constitutive of, the actions we carry out. They are done knowledgeably, but without necessarily being available to the discursive awareness of the actor. To speak a language, an individual needs to know an enormously complicated range of rules, strategies and tactics involved in language use. However, if that individual were asked to give a discursive account of what it is that he or she knows in knowing these rules, etc., he or she would normally find it very difficult indeed. Any analysis of social activity which ignores practical consciousness is massively deficient." (Giddens (1987) Social Theory and Modern Sociology, Cambridge: Polity Press, p.63).*

reproduction: it relates micro-discursive activities to macro-social structures. The built environment in which we operate, the laws and rules that govern our behaviour, the associations of power and influence that are inscribed in our relationships, the established conventions, manners and agreements that shape our contacts with each other, etc. all have structural qualities (are stable for periods) that have a social impact on us all. These structural aspects of society are ever-present; they are features of the social world in which we live and work and they continue to exist through time; they are, in other words, constantly being reproduced as macro-structures. But as they are reproduced they are changed in line with the myriad of micro-decisions that people make individually and collectively.

When established ways of doing things alter (and they always do) institutions change. Structuration theory allows for an analysis of institutional change that recognises the part played by the understandings, attitudes and actions of those knowledgeable actors who, in the context of a particular institutional setting, engage in continuous dialogue. It is this emphasis on engagement and dialogue that points to the significance of 'discourse' in social reproduction and incremental transformation. In other words, the repeated habitual acts of individual agents create and reproduce the structures within which they function. Social and institutional change has to be seen as a complex subtle thing brought about by how people think, talk and act. Our engagement with others has consequences. What we say and how we behave alters the structural settings within which we operate: when we make decisions or habitually behave differently we change both institutions and institutional arrangements.

In these essays we emphasise the basic tenet of multiple rationality analysis that says: by engaging with the discourse, knowledgeable actors have the capacity to transform it. In our discussions we take a view of 'discourse' that goes beyond (or breaks from) restricted linguistic or logical categories so as to allow a mode of discourse analysis that is capable of investigating the totality of all statements in their dispersion as events. We might say that social history is simply the story of human engagement. This critical way of viewing things is essentially a structurationist approach in that it regards discourse as being embedded in social practices and institutions, and treats the 'events' as 'statements' that are constituted by the everyday actions of knowledgeable actors. This knowledgeability goes beyond knowing syntactical rules - it embraces mastery of the circumstances in which language is acted out in social interaction. It involves the mutual coordination of language and praxis[30] - or as the social historian Michel Foucault put it - the development of institutions and institutional practices involves "dispositions, manoeuvres, tactics, techniques, functionings....."[31], so that a knowledgeable actor has not merely mastered sets of syntactical and semantic rules, but the wide, complex and subtle range of conventions that he or she may find difficult or impossible to explain but which are nevertheless 'known' at the level of practical consciousness and which play a key part in the functioning of day-to-day social activity.

Any notion of 'discourse' inevitably carries connotations of 'dialogue', and as we have already argued, effective dialogue involves the fixing of some degree of shared meaning to the statements and activities that constitute the discourse. This was the very point Wittgenstein was making with his notion of forms of life. Critical social theory both extends and explicates Wittgenstein's argument. It extends it in two ways: firstly by moving the analysis beyond an examination of the structure of language and

[30] See Ira J Cohen, 'Structuration Theory and Social Praxis', in Giddens A and Turner J (1987) Social Theory Today, Cambridge: Polity Press, pp.273.

[31] Foucault M (1979) Discipline and Punish: The Birth of the Prison. London: Penguin Edition (Peregrine).

the nature of spoken and written encounters; and secondly by embracing everything that signifies or has meaning in discursive encounters. It explicates Wittgenstein's insight by developing the concept of inter-subjectivity. Both aspects of this reformulation will be explored in what follows.

The Tyranny of Common Sense

"The maxims of men reveal their characters." (Luc De Vauvanargues)

No popular idea ever has a single origin. But the idea that the sole purpose of a company is to make money for its shareholders was given prominence in an article by the influential economist Milton Friedman in the New York Times on September 13, 1970. Friedman's article was uncompromising. It argued that any business executives who pursued a goal other than making money were "unwitting puppets of the intellectual forces that have been undermining the basis of a free society these past decades." They were, he argued, guilty of "analytical looseness and lack of rigour." Ironically, the article made a series of loose assertions, some of which might be regarded as more ideological than analytical. Friedman suggested that investing in community projects (or anything other than corporate interests) should be regarded as "undemocratic". Executives with wider community commitments, he argued, had become "unelected government officials" who were illegally taxing employers and customers. The article began with the bold assertion that in a free enterprise, private-property system, it is a self-evident truth "requiring no justification" that a corporate executive is an employee of the owners of the business - namely the shareholders.

Milton Friedman presented controversial views as 'common sense'.

How did the Nobel prize winner arrive at these conclusions? Friedman was making the classic mistake of which we are all guilty at various times. He addressed a debateable proposition through the distorting lens of his own presuppositions and then presented his views as 'common sense'. There are numerous examples of this tendency but arguably one of the most extreme was his blunt statement that "the Great Depression, like most other periods of severe unemployment, was produced by government mismanagement rather than by any inherent instability of the private economy".[33] Friedman's logic hinged on an implied assertion that western democracies should abandon the idea of the mixed economy in favour of social and economic arrangements that are unequivocally capitalist in nature. If this is not the case - and many would argue that it isn't - then his assertions are a reflection of a personal conviction rather than a statement of fact.

How we think and talk about current affairs depends in great part upon when and where we live. Milton Friedman, the son of Jewish immigrants, was born in Brooklyn, New York in 1912. He was very much a man of his time and his monetarist theories were influential in the corridors of power of his day. In the early 1980s both the Reagan and Thatcher administrations used his teachings to justify their socio-economic policies of deregulation, low taxation and cuts in public spending. Some sixteen years after the publication of his piece in the New York Times the world was plunged into a protracted monetary crisis that has subsequently resulted in a great deal of critical comment about the inward-looking and short-term policies of banks and other corporate entities. Following the global crisis, new attitudes emerged that pointed to the need for more effective regulation and a general rethinking about the relationship between business and society. Opinion has now shifted and today it would be difficult to find many political or business leaders who unequivocally subscribe to Friedman's trenchant views. In particular, recent research carried out by Harvard and other leading business schools indicates that Friedman's assumed fault line segregating corporate and community interests is illusionary. [See Appendix 1 'Shared Value']

Unanalysed[34] opinions based on convictions can be problematic – particularly when those opinions are instrumental in steering important policy decisions. Nietzsche argued that we should be wary of having the courage of our convictions and that true intellectual courage is better demonstrated when we show a willingness to have our convictions challenged. John Stuart Mill made a similar point when he argued that if we want to understand an issue, we

*[33] https://www.brainyquote.com/quotes/milton_friedman_*

[34] The word "unanalyzed" rather than "unchallenged" is used for reasons that will become clear as our argument unfolds.

have to begin by learning the grounds of our own opinions.[35] For most of us there would seem to be something psychologically hard wired into our approach to argument and debate that ordinarily makes us more eager to search out reasons for justifying what we already think and say about society than for reasons that might lead us to think differently and change our opinions. Indeed, it would seem that in arguments the presentation of facts that challenge an already established opinion sometimes acts to force a face-saving reconfirmation of a challenged point of view. If this is a problem (and we are here arguing that it is), then it is a problem that has been intensified by the development and growth of information technology and social networks that allow us to self-select our intellectual engagement to a restricted range of ideas and opinions. Some commentators suggest that the extensive use of social networking means that we are increasingly living in personalised 'information bubbles' in which our entrenched opinions are continuously reinforced and alternative points of view are consciously and systematically dismissed as "false" or simply excluded.

Whereas 'social media' is a way of transmitting or sharing information with a broad audience, 'social networking' is an act of engagement. Groups of people with common interests or like-minds, associate together on social networking sites and build relationships. In 2016, it was estimated that some forty per cent of the US population got its news from Facebook. Global social networking sites probably have well in excess of 2 billion monthly users (2019).

In the world of politics and corporate affairs, statements that are presented as 'objective' and proposals that are proffered as 'rational' are often embedded in value and interest judgements. Legal and commercial privileges are put forward as being in the public or corporate interest, personal gain is justified by reference to the inevitable (and legitimate) forces of supply and demand, and political ideologies pretend to be immutable economic laws. Put simply, in public life subjective arguments are often presented as disinterested principles, and opinions masquerade as truths "requiring no justification". When these distortions occur in the context of policy discussions they can result in decisions that the decision-makers themselves eventually live to regret.

[35] *J.S.Mill (1859) On Liberty, Chapter 2: 'On the Liberty of Thought and Discussion'.*

Common sense is not enough

Experts in risk management stress the importance of correcting avoidable errors during the processes of strategic thinking and planning. The problem is that the tools offered for this task are largely derived from economics and finance rather than from philosophy and psychology and by operating within the limits of cost-benefit and probability analysis, they are ill-equipped to tackle problems derived from competing rationalities. What is missing is a systematic approach to policy formation that helps to rectify misperceptions, refute false assumptions, reconcile conflicting opinions, and question 'common sense' assertions.

A commitment to analyse our own and other people's ways of rationalising propositions is more of an attitude than a technique. It is an attitude that seeks to incorporate into policy making an awareness of the distorting effects of both poor communication and human attitudes and interests. Rationality analysis has two primary objectives. First it seeks to make policy discussions more coherent by clarifying differences in the understandings of both contested and essentially contested concepts.[36] Second, it seeks to make policy discussions more comprehensive by identifying the multiplicity of goals associated with any particular policy proposal. The operational logic underpinning this way of looking at things is that an analysis of value justifications should be part of the strategic thinking that precedes decision planning, implementation and management.

Talking common sense

Given the book's declared commitment to fully thought-through strategic analysis, the reader might be forgiven for thinking that its attitude towards common sense thinking and the use of common sense expressions is entirely negative. This is not the case and any such presumption would constitute a misreading of the argument. Common sense assertions become dangerous only when they are used as a substitute for thinking. In most forms of human communication (whether domestic, social, confrontational, academic, pedagogic, scientific, artistic, business, philosophical or journalistic) we usefully summarise, clarify or emphasise our points of view by employing allusions, analogies, metaphors and aphoris-

[36] These terms are explained and discussed in chapter 3

tic sayings of various kinds. To be forbidden to do so would not only impoverish our speaking and writing, it would make the very process of communicating difficult and in some instances impossible.

In these essays we argue that assumed social truths reside in how we talk about things (the 'discourse') not in the things we talk about (the 'subjects' of discourse). To put it succinctly: social truth is relative to discourse.[37]
Some communicative distortions are 'innocent' and stem from an individual's lack of self-knowledge. Often communicative distortions are not 'innocent' but knowingly deliberate misrepresentations that are asserted with the intention of reinforcing a predetermined position. This form of 'cynical' distortion might involve such techniques as the selective use of statistics, the making of dubious cause and effect connections and false analogies – more of this later.

Although as we have already argued in the Introduction, not all communication is language based, it clearly forms the source of most discursive activities and it is the primary communication tool used by those engaged in dialogue and interactive decision-making. The various ways in which language is consciously and unconsciously manipulated in the interest of an argument is one of the themes running through this book. Later we will consider how appeals to 'common sense' are all too often used to circumvent the 'deep thinking' necessary to formulate sustainable policies. This is a complex subject and we will start, quite simply, by drawing attention to the fact that common sense sayings of various kinds populate much of our spoken and written communication. This fact indicates the existence of an important relationship between language use and common sense thinking.

Common-sense observations and assertions tend to be phrase-wrapped in ways that make them accessible and memorable. These common sense sayings are categorised by grammarians in a variety of ways so that it becomes possible to distinguish between a maxim, an adage, a truism, an aphorism, a proverb, etc. There

[37] The twentieth century idea of 'communicative distortion' emerged from the long-standing debate about relativism.

exist an unusually high number of English language words describing sayings of this kind: we could have added idiom, apothegm, epigram, cliché, and several others to the list. The number of such linguistic structures highlights how common sense sayings are deeply embedded in our language culture. More importantly (for our discussion) we need to consider what such linguistic structures have in common.

Recourse to common sense in dialogue or debate is both necessary and dangerous and it is constantly called upon to support arguments. Indeed, it is often used not simply to illustrate or support an argument, but to assert a not-to-be-questioned reality. The mere claim to "be" common sense is often used to assert that a particular claim to truth does not need to be rationalised because its veracity is self-evident or it is for some other reason pre-established. In this way, common sense can be used to curtail an argument or to make a generalisation that has not been worked for intellectually.

For a dogmatist, finding the truth is like looking for an elephant in a haystack – it is simply obvious and does not need to be discussed.

By establishing a proposition as "common sense" further arguments for its acceptance are deemed to be unnecessary. The appeal to common sense is meant to allow a proposition to be accepted without the proposer having to confront those logical and philosophical barriers that arise from factual or interpretative uncertainties. Criticism of this tendency does not suggest that in complex arguments generalisations cannot be made: it does imply, however, that to be legitimate, they have to be "worked for". Although it can act as a succinct summing up of a rationalised position, common sense is not a substitute for creative thinking or rational argument.

Throughout this book we will consciously employ a large number of sayings of an aphoristic or proverbial nature. They have been employed partly to make the point that the use of pithy quotations in serious discourse is absolutely legitimate. In such a context their function is to capture attention, compress a point of view, encapsulate an argument, summarise an idea, or simplify a complex thought. However, this form of textual embellishment is no more than a discursive device. Like any tool it can be misused and, in any event, its use is limited. To argue that 'the proverb is the truth' is as sensible as arguing that 'the logo is the firm', 'the title is the poem', 'the trailer is the film', or 'the cover is the book'.

Aphorisms have a sort of rhythmic power – they enable a poignant point to be poetically put. Despite its pretence to wisdom, an epigrammatic assertion should never be seen as a 'self-evident truth'. To make this point in a proverbial fashion, we might say that social truth is relative to discourse and dependent on context. Of course, this proposed new proverb should not be taken at face value: the next few chapters will examine what it might mean and we will "work" to justify its veracity. We will begin by considering the dangers of relying on common sense thinking and talking when making important decisions.

The limits of common sense

Albert Einstein is reported to have said that "common sense is nothing more than a deposit of prejudices laid down by the mind before you reach eighteen."[38] Einstein's comment was intended to highlight the relationship between common sense statements and the cultural background

[38] Attributed to Albert Einstein in Mathematics, Queen and Servant of the Sciences (1952) by Eric Temple Bell.

from which they emerge. The notion of common sense as a cultural phenomenon was famously considered by Antonio Gramsci who, in using the term, broadly meant it to refer to the set of generally held assumptions and propositional beliefs about social life that are common to a specific group within a society. He variously described it as “the philosophy of non-philosophers”, “spontaneous philosophy”, or “the folklore of philosophy”[39] By the use of such phrases he attempted to distinguish common sense from the more theoretical ways of rationalising employed by intellectuals. Following Gramsci, we might say that common sense is the traditional, popular conception of the world for a particular social community at a particular time and it represents the milieu in which philosophical trends and social assumptions become popularly understood.

Everyday communications inevitably take place in the context of more or less common sense ideas and assumptions. Anyone who sought constantly to abandon the common sense assumptions of his or her community and get through the daily transactions of life by thinking, behaving and speaking like an academic philosopher would probably go mad or be sectioned under the mental health legislation as though they were mad; at the very least, they would be labelled as strange and eccentric. Common sense beliefs and assumptions constitute a form of operational philosophy that allows for the smooth running of day-to-day living. They facilitate inconsequential, routine interactivity and thereby allow for the creation of a shared conception of everyday meanings that makes daily, collaborative social life possible.

As a value system, it might be argued that common sense provides a moral frame of reference for the concrete experiences of everyday life. Indeed, to the extent that it is based on practical experience, common sense carries a degree of authority. However, because of its mundane nature, it is unlikely to be a satisfactory arbitrator when multi-faceted technical, ethical or political disagreements occur. As a source of authority it has some discursive purchase but little intellectual credibility. Throughout this book we argue that the reliability of any generalisation that has not been worked for intellectually should be challenged and that those making impor-

[39] Gramsci A, (1971), p.149.

tant policy decisions should avoid uncritically accepting a point of view that has been simply absorbed from the local culture as a down-to-earth statement of 'how things are'.

As a system of thought common sense does not involve critical awareness but rather it tends to involve a comprehension of the world that is uncritically taken from, or is imposed by, the external environment. That is, from or by one of the various cultural communities with which people are involved from the moment they enter the conscious world. This implies that what is counted as common sense by one group of people may not be regarded as such by some other group.

> *"In acquiring one's conception of the world one always belongs to a particular grouping which is that of all the social elements which share the same mode of thinking and acting."(Gramsci 1971, p.324)*

Although common sense allows for categorisation and thereby for something to become an object of perception, because of its unself-critical nature, it cannot be regarded as logical in a universal and strictly philosophical sense."[40]
As John Stuart Mill put it,
"Popular opinions, on subjects not palpable to sense, are often true, but seldom or never the whole truth".[41]
Common sense fails to operate under what critical theorists refer to as 'ideal speech conditions'.[42]

Anthony Giddens suggests that to get at the essence of common sense and to understand its properties, it has to be distinguished from what he terms 'mutual knowledge'. Within any recognisable culture, or what Giddens refers to as a "speech community", people share common frames of reference in order to make themselves understood. This 'mutual knowledge' is the routine, taken-for-granted background awareness that facilitates everyday social order and interaction. It is a pre-existing stock of overlapping shared cultural understandings from which

[40] Because the notion of 'ideal speech' is (by tautological definition) an idealized one, operational, everyday arrangements are always more or less imperfect relative to the 'ideal' (see chapter 7 for further discussion on this point).

[41] J S Mill (1859), On Liberty, chapter 2.

[42] See chapter 6.

people (including those subscribing to opposing common sense opinions) draw in order to make themselves understood.[43] It is a reflection of the established, socially sanctioned way of doing things in the everyday social world. It is, in short, our knowledge of how to get along in the world. It is a form of practical consciousness that constitutes the knowledge of what to do. By establishing ways of behaving and allowing meaning to be sustained through interaction, mutual knowledge frames, but does not determine, common sense propositions: it determines the socially acceptable ways in which common sense is communicated. In other words, mutual knowledge is not common sense but the vehicle through which common sense propositions are communicated. To make an analogy - western composers share a mutual understanding of the established traditions and rules of composition but often create their own very distinctive pieces of music.

Common sense is something fundamentally different from mutual knowledge. Indeed, common sense is not treated by Giddens as knowledge at all, but as "fallible belief". The distinction between mutual knowledge and common sense is really a distinction between understanding and belief.[44] If we assume that you and I reside in a common culture (society), we will both draw on the same sources of definitions and frames of reference when interacting. Despite this, my common sense belief of what is right or wrong in a particular situation - what is or is not efficacious, what is fair or unfair, what is worthwhile or a waste of time, etc. - may differ from yours. In terms of decision-making or policy formation we will both use the same broad frameworks of understanding but, in so doing, we may appeal to different rationality principles. In short, mutual knowledge allows you and me to share an understanding that we disagree: we both understand that my common sense belief of what to do differs from yours.[45]

[43] It is the result of cumulative prior social activity and is not solipsistic.

[44] A distinction that in a different literature is mirrored by the analysis of how the differences between the notions of 'shared cognition' and a 'collective mindset' are understood. That is, how to distinguish the nature of overlapping knowledge structures from the process of how individuals in groups come to think alike in a specific context.

[45] This idea of 'an agreed disagreement' is central to rationality analysis as developed in subsequent chapters.

The key characteristic of a common sense assertion is that its lacks self-critical awareness – 'it's true because it's true'. An important question that has to be addressed is: 'Does the uncritical nature of common sense mean that it is devoid of all rationality?' The anthropologist Clifford Geertz has considered the uncritical nature of common sense. In his essay 'Common Sense as a Cultural System'[46] Geertz argues (p.75) that although common sense may not be reflective, it is not devoid of considered thought: it does allow for criticism of a kind; it is capable of being critical - but not self-critical. In other words, common sense may not display the intellectual rigour and concrete methodological features of bodies of scholastic knowledge such as physics, economics and jurisprudence, nor may it display the relatively stable perspective and revelatory claims of religious or ideological systems of thought and belief such as Christianity, Islam, Marxism or Existentialism: but nevertheless, it is more than a random, arbitrary and completely volatile arrangement of thought, opinion and attitude. This means that common sense is more than random non-deliberated views about the world, unshackled from anything systematic and tied only to the ever-changing life-experiences of individual subjects. Like religion, science or ideology, common sense might be thought of as having authority: however – and this is the point - we need to be aware of the limits of such authority and the dangers of pursuing courses of action based upon it.

Common sense knowledge carries with it more than a self-evident down-to-earth appreciation that something is as it is: like other cultural systems, it also carries implied assumptions about 'right action'. When common sense tells us something worldly about what fire can do to human flesh or what being out in the rain can do to health or the consequences of getting addicted to heroine, that knowledge carries with it unspoken assertions about the nature of common sense actions. The authority for such assertions is powerful precisely because it comes from the world of experience. In other words, a matter-of-fact appreciation of the way things are, leads to down-to-earth judgements or assessments of how best to act. In short, it leads to what Geertz terms "colloquial wisdom".

[46] Geertz C (1983), Local Knowledge, Further Essays in Interpretive Anthropology, New York: Basic Books.

> *"When we say someone shows common sense we mean to suggest more than that he is just using his eyes and ears, but is, as we say, keeping them open, using them judiciously, intelligently, perceptively, reflectively, or trying to, and that he is capable of coping with everyday problems with some effectiveness."*
> *(Geertz. p.76)*

Common sense is thought of as being synonymous with experience: it is how we talk about experience. It is because common sense is thought of as a 'matter-of-fact' interpretation of experience that it has the authority it does. It constitutes a frame of reference for the concrete experiences of life. As a frame of thought it is like any religion, science or philosophy in that it claims to reach past illusion to 'truth' - to 'things as they are'. As an account of what is, it claims for itself an authority by striking at the heart of self-evident reality through an appeal to the immediacies of 'Everyman's experience'. Geertz, however, makes the point that common sense interpretations and judgements are localised 'matters-of-fact'.

> *"Anthropology can be of use here in much the same way as it is generally: providing out-of-the-way cases, it sets nearby ones in an altered context."*
> *(ibid. p.77)*

In his illustrative example, Geertz compares and contrasts judgements of and reactions to hermaphroditism in three different societies. He argues that received ideas of what is 'natural' and 'normal' differ considerably so that common sense reactions to intersexuality range from horror and nausea at a self-evident 'misfortune' in America to wonder and awe at a self-evident 'blessing' among the Navaho, and to a kind of indifference at a self-evident 'mistake' within the East African Pokot tribe. In short, common sense is not what the mind clear of cant spontaneously apprehends; it is what the mind filled with presuppositions - that sex is a disorganizing force, that sex is a regenerative gift, that sex is a practical pleasure - concludes. "God may have made the intersexuals, but man has made the rest."(ibid. p.84)

Accepting Geertz's critique that common sense conclusions vary radically from one place and time to the next leaves open the question of what it is that gives common sense its transcultural character. Geertz concludes that what unites systems of common sense whose contents differ is a common 'voice'.

> *"Like the voice of piety, the voice of sanity sounds pretty much the same whatever it says; what simple wisdom has everywhere in common is the maddening air of simple wisdom with which it is uttered."*
> *(ibid. p.85)*

When and wherever it appears, the common sense voice presents itself as being natural, practical, simple, accessible and non-contentious. By harnessing these quasi-qualities common sense statements seek to avoid (or even veto) debate. What unifies common sense as a system of thought across cultures is not common conclusions but a similarity of mood, tone and temper. It is for this reason that Geertz analyses common sense in terms of its apparent quasi-qualities rather than in terms of its content or methodology. This is a significant point because it explains why there can be occasions when we are not so much won over by an argument we can analyse, but rather by the tone and temper in which an argument is put.

Using Mary Douglas's distinction between 'dirty' and 'clean', Robert Wuthnow et al amplify the above by making the point that common sense injunctions are more than purely cognitive issues or matters of location.

"It is not that scraps of food are clean when on the plate and dirty when on the table, but that they should be on the plate and not on the table. There is a moral dimension to reality that makes the question of classification, and misclassification, also a question of right and wrong. The moral order is coterminous with social reality such that things have at one and the same time a factual and a moral existence. When we say 'that is the way things are', we are not only making a factual statement about the mechanical appropriateness of nature, but a moral evaluation of that order." (Cultural Analysis 1984, p.87. In Wuthnall R el al.

The work of other cultural anthropologists such as Peter Berger and Mary Douglas make the point that our taken-for-granted common sense reality is socially constructed so that shared understandings about what is 'right action' carry more than reasoned analysis of why it is sensible to act in a particular way - it carries a distinctly moral charge. The overt "why" is intrinsically associated with a more hidden 'should'. Common sense judgements are part of the structure (what Berger refers to as the 'sacred canopy')[47] of the symbolic universes within which we interact, so that common sense statements imply a social reality such that things and social arrangements have an apparent factual existence that is underpinned by a moral imperative.

The argument we are making here is that common sense can be (and often is) referenced as a system of thought justifying practical and moral propositions in ways that turn debateable claims to truth (right action) into self-evident statements of what is the 'right thing to do'. Herein lies its potential for tyranny.

[47] See Berger P (1967), The Sacred Canopy, New York: Doubleday.

Chapter 3

Ambiguity

"The world is messy and full of ambiguities" (Barak Obama 27 October 2019)

The ambiguity of words

Weasels suck out the content of a bird's egg through a small hole in the shell leaving the egg appearing intact, but of course having no potential for life. Weasel words and phrases are expressions that have vague, 'empty-shell' meanings but are nevertheless employed by speakers wishing to give the impression that what they are saying has substance (is meaningful and authoritative). The uncritical use of such imprecise words and phrases appeals to simple, unquestioning common sense for its authority rather than to testable evidence. In political and commercial discourses the employment of such words and terms seeks to give the appearance of real content whilst protecting the speaker from the need to provide supporting evidence or a fully rationalised argument. In some cases their use constitutes a conscious attempt to protect the proposer from being held to account or from legal redress. The vague and anonymous nature of this ambiguous authority allows those employing such words to deny any specific meaning in the event of their proffered statements being subsequently challenged. Although the use of this sort of disingenuous language is particularly prevalent in party political argument and commercial advertising, it also permeates all sorts of other professional and popular discourses.

The Scottish enlightenment philosopher Thomas Reid argued that there is no greater impediment to the advancement of knowledge than the ambiguity of words. To make an obvious point, words have to be used in discourse for meanings to emerge. Dictionaries define simple word meanings but they cannot define the precise, more socially refined, meanings that arise from discourse. Because the same word can take on different meanings in different contexts, we might say that word meanings are relative to discourse. This need for context (language use rather than word definition) is well illustrated by a story about what happens when simple word translation is relied upon to impart the meaning of an enigmatic phrase. Traceable back to the cold war days of the1960s, this apocryphal tale concerned the use of a computer program commissioned by the CIA. It was designed to make instant translations between English and Russian. To test the program, it was decided to use it to translate a well-known phrase into Russian and then translate the result back into English to see if the word structure and its meaning survived the exercise. The Head of the CIA was invited to carry out the test and the development team watched expectantly as he typed in his chosen test piece: "Out of sight, out of mind". The computer took its time and everyone was beginning to fear that the program had failed to function when suddenly the spools of magnetic tape began to whirl and the early golf ball printer clattered out the result: **"Invisible insanity"**.

When words are devoid of a context they are footloose and untethered from intent. By contrast, in discourse words not only take on refined meanings, but they also become purposeful. This means that in discourse language is not neutral and words are more than cyphers and signifiers. Language philosophers in the broad pragmatist tradition make this point particularly strongly. Writers such as Richard Rorty, Humberto Maturana and Daniel Dennett for example, suggest that, post Darwin, we can start thinking of language in biological as well as in socio-philosophical terms.

That is, language can be seen as a survival resource in which words act as tools that are used to pursue particular interests and deal with the dangers and opportunities presented by the environment (rather than simply representing the intrinsic nature of that environment).

Words and phrases can be recruited to support a political cause or be used to undermine objective thinking. During the increasingly violent protests against the war in Vietnam, the obfuscating phrase "collateral damage" was famously recruited to the US Administration's vocabulary in an attempt to maintain public support for continuing the war. It fooled virtually nobody as most Americans knew only too well that it was a weasel phrase replacing the more starkly honest "civilian casualties" - and the protests continued. In our own time politically charged phrases are constantly dropped into public debates about contentious issues. To give but one clear example, it was noticeable that those campaigning for Britain's withdrawal from the European Union tended to refer to European professional government administrators as "unelected faceless bureaucrats" whilst labelling their British counterparts "civil servants".

Specific words and phrases are not 'weasely' per se – to be classified as such, their use has to embrace an intention to deceive or mislead. Weasel words cover a range of different discourse-distorting speech elements. Some critics of this practice have attempted to classify weasel words into different types. A 2009 study suggested that the majority of weasel words used by contributors to Wikipedia could be divided into three broad categories.[48] The first uses adverbs and adjectives to qualify statements. These have the effect of softening the force of a potentially loaded assertion by subtly modifying an otherwise bold claim to truth. Their inclusion, particularly in written documents, allows for future disclaimers to be made when things do not turn out as predicted. Examples of such quietly placed 'escape hatch' words and phrases include "often", "normally", "probably", "usually", "in most respects", "typically", "somewhat", "expected". The second type takes the form of numerically vague expressions such as "some people", "experts", "many", etc. The third type makes use of the passive

[48] https://en.wikipedia.org/wiki/Weasel_word#cite_note-14

voice to avoid specifying an authority. By using phrases such as "it is said that", "it would seem to be" or "there is general agreement that" the speaker implies, but fails to specify, some authority in

I remember some years ago listening to the conservative philosopher Roger Scruton debating a policy issue with a more liberally orientated academic (whose name escapes me). They were considering the efficacy of increasing public spending on the NHS. Scruton was making the point that spending more money is seldom the best way to enhance welfare outcomes. To reinforce his argument, he drew an analogy between current household spending on food and the significantly lower amount spent during the Second World War. His argument was that evidence suggests that during the War when diets were severely restricted, the general health of the nation was higher. In reply, his protagonist suggested that equating the consequences of a restricted war-time diet with limiting the investment in the quantity and quality of modern health care facilities was inappropriate. In reply to her, the professor agreed that the analogy might not be exact but it made his point. In return, she then replied, "If the analogy falls, the argument falls". To this he had no answer.

order to enhance the credibility of a contestable claim. To be clear, the use of such qualifying or generalised terms can be perfectly legitimate in open discussion and argument – and indeed is inevitable in everyday speech. Such phrases only become weasel words when their inclusion is made consciously knowing that the claim to truth is doubtful, or there is an intention to give an exaggerated impression of a statement's veracity. Motivation and intent lie behind, and are integral to, the creation of weasel words and phrases.

Language analysts have always been aware of the tendency for vague or illogical argument to be employed in certain discursive situations and this has led to the formal recognition of a number of linguistic constructs employed either to distort the discourse or make it 'safely' dysfunctional. These grammatical devices include the use of non-sequiturs and euphemisms, both of which have the effect of inhibiting rational argument. In public debate non-sequiturs are constantly slipped into the sequencing of an argument in the form of false analogies. Similarly, euphemisms are often cast into the debate in the form of incomprehensible gobbledegook, management speak or other types of jargon. All of these devices distort the dialogue and work against clarity of argument. When they are used with the intention to confuse, they can be classified as weasel words.

Arguments of course, take the form of statements rather than single words or phrases. 'Empty shell' statements that are designed to manipulate policy discussions are often presented as interesting stories rather than as bland, testable, objective, probability assessments. Both the tone and content of these vivid, easily understood narratives often possess fairy tale qualities that grab the attention. When someone begins their argument about the consequences of a proposed policy with a phrase such as "I remember years ago my mother telling me....; "I used to live in France and I can tell you that the French way of doing things is....";"This argument reminds me of the time that I.....'; or "I was talking to someone who used to work for....."; etc.; we know that we are in for a once upon a time story rather than a piece of reasoned, checkable analysis. Anecdotal stories are used to underpin unverifiable generalisations and they play a crucial role in the production of crude stereotypes. Also they are arguably an effective way of replacing expert opinion with the common sense of the common man (or the wise old mother). Moralising stories are particularly appealing to those who dislike complex arguments and are seeking simple certainties rather than difficult multi-rational understandings.

NOTE

In some respects we seem to have evolved as a narrative species. Until recently we pursued knowledge and understanding largely through the telling of stories based on actual or fantasised experiences. Jag Bhalla recently likened the need for story telling to Steven Pinker's notion of 'the language instinct' - arguing that an inborn hunger for story hearing and story making emerges untutored in all healthy children and that "every culture bathes their children in stories to explain how the world works and to engage and educate their emotions". (Guest Blog in Scientific American on 8 May 2013). Arguably, it was not until the Enlightenment that we were able to refer to a secular body of non-anecdotal 'authentic' knowledge as a reference upon which to base our propositions and validate our claims to truth.

There is an old saying that 'every difficult problem has a simple solution – and it's always wrong'. The law of requisite variety[49] attempts to intellectualise this piece of folksy spontaneous philosophy. The so-called law states that only variety can absorb variety - which means that when confronted with a complex (high variety) challenge, the best way to solve it is to bring in an equal amount of variety to bear down upon it. This is done by convening a range of special advisers (the so called 'requisite variety of individuals') who, by virtue of their combined knowledge, experience, expertise and influence are well equipped to deal with the challenge. This may seem to be rather an obvious decision-making strategy but it is a relatively recent introduction into management thinking and is designed to counteract the perceived tendency to employ specialist consultants who claim to be decision experts but whose knowledge is, in reality, restricted to highly specific modelling techniques and who reference only a narrow range of professional experiences.

THE AMBIGUITY OF 'BEST PRACTICE'

When the underlying logic of various policy proposals is not given proper consideration, arguments will not have been properly tested. The resulting impoverishment of the decision discourse will increase the likelihood of the final decision being unsustainable.

One of the key tenets of what we are terming *multiple rationality analysis* is that 'generalisations are acceptable only if they have been worked for'.[50] The Golden Rule of multiple rationality analysis is that when putting forward a point of view that claims to be rational, we need to "specify and quantify". This principle will be explored in detail in later chapters. For the time being, we will simply make the point that in policy debates opinions tend to be more readily available than the reasons for holding those opinions.

On the face of it, many purely technical problems would appear to have unambiguous, commonsensical 'best' solutions. In such fields

[49] A term coined by Ross Ashby. This notion is analogous to the notion of 'the truth of experience' in the standard philosophy literature.

[50] For a fuller discussion of this point see Garnett D (1999), 'Absent Voices: Accommodating the Interests of Future Generations Through Multiple Rationality Analysis', in the International Journal of Sustainable Development, Vol.2, No.4.

as medical science and engineering, for example, we might expect a high degree of agreement about what counts as 'best practice'. However, the more we look into it, the more it becomes apparent that even in scientifically orientated fields, what counts as an appropriate action is not as clear as one might at first expect: in science and technology, as in most things, 'context counts'. There is, for example, no simple answer to the question 'What's the best way to build a bridge?' The answer would largely depend on how much money was available for its construction and what it is to be used for. The location of the bridge in time and space will influence its design: its intended use and its location will bring to the fore questions about safety, aesthetics, future maintenance costs, etc. Another way of making this point is to say that when placed in a particular commissioning context, engineering rationality has to confront other rationalities tied to other disciplines such as economics, politics, sociology, ergonomics and law, etc.

The multiplicity of rationalities becomes particularly apparent when we are dealing with social and community decision-making where such notions as fiscal fairness, social returns, equal opportunities, inter-generational justice, anti-social behaviour, environmental damage, etc. might need to be addressed. The potential for a clash of rationalities becomes more apparent still when we recognise that underlying these different disciplinary and socio-political attitudes, there exists the differing values, cultural beliefs and personal agendas of individual decision-makers and those influencing them.

In looking back at earlier social policy decisions, hindsight judgement shows that some important decisions are regretted in retrospect.[51] What gets done depends in large part on people's attitudes, predispositions and opinions about what is right action. It is problematic when duplicitous, insincere people manipulate decision discourses to achieve outcomes that they know are not in the general interest; but it is also problematic when well-meaning, decent people use their influence to contribute to errors of

[51] This assertion is based on research interviews I carried out with local government officers as part of the CARM Project (Condition Appraisal and Renewal Management) in the 1990s (University of the West of England). Refer: Garnett D (2006) Building Obsolescence: The Theory and Practice of Building Renewal, Faculty of the Built Environment, UWE Bristol. [Republished 2016 in 'Housing' leapingfrogpublications.co.uk]

collective judgement. When it comes to policy-making, neither the sincere nor the insincere are neutral. As Goethe famously said, "I can promise to be sincere, but I cannot promise to be impartial."[52] In modern democracies, policy ideas compete with each other for enactment in what we might term the market place of propositions. This quasi market has a number of locations including political manifestos, popular media outlets, pressure group activities, scholarly publications, committee meetings, teaching syllabuses, and debating chambers. It is a feature of competition that a particular product emerges (albeit temporarily) as dominant in the market place: as with products so also with ideas and social policies. The conditions of effective democracy in governing arrangements are analogous to the conditions of perfect competition in economic arrangements - and so long as democratic conditions are maintained, new ideas can emerge and be given voice to challenge the existing order.[53] The conditions of effective democracy might be assumed to include free elections, an ability and inclination to check facts, an open education system, a willingness to change policies in the light of new information or changed circumstances and, just as important, freedom of thought and speech.[54]

It is generally understood that participants in democratically orientated policy debates tend to hold on to their starting arguments doggedly and can remain generally impervious to rationalisations (or even factual evidence) that may challenge the assumptions behind their proposals. It is often personal experience rather than intellectual argument that changes opinions. A change in thinking often occurs in response to specific events or altered circumstances such as a loss of a chief executive, complaint from a major customer, harsher loan conditions being imposed by a lender, the threat of a terrorist outrage, an unanticipated tragedy, the success of a political opponent in a by-election, etc.

Just as it is often experience rather than interpersonal debate

[52] Reported by Fairbain F.M. (1890), Religion in History and in the Life of Today, London and New York: Hodder & Stoughton.

[53] Just as in free enterprise markets, so long as the conditions of competition exist, new products and services can arise to challenge the current market leaders.

[54] We will later argue (crucially) that 'freedom of thought' is different from 'emancipated thought' and 'freedom of expression' is different from 'undistorted discourse'.

that tends to lead individuals to shift their entrenched opinions about social and political policy, so it is with decision groups. It

Devil in the detail

is said that when it comes to major changes to government or corporate policy, "the devil's in the detail". In many cases it might be better to argue that "the imps are in the implementation".[55] Often, during the period of consultation preceding the introduction of a policy change, civil servants, practitioners and academic commentators point to both ethical objections and practical problems. Although such criticisms may influence the nature or scope of the final enactment, resultant modifications typically bring about small-scale negotiated compromises rather than major reassessments of the proposal's fundamentals. However, more significant modifications can, in the end, be belatedly introduced once real and immediate practical difficulties become apparent during the process of implementation. All too often, the full negative implications of a policy change are only taken seriously when decision-makers or their agents are charged with the responsibility of implementation. Having said this, even when serious difficulties are highlighted during the piloting of policies, there can be a tendency for politicians and executive managers to 'stick to their guns' and rationalise the problems as being due to "special local conditions" or "early adjustment issues".[56] When flawed policies are grounded in the ideological presuppositions of politicians or the fixed presumptions of top executives, it can be the case that no amount of argument or piloting will persuade instigators to draw back from their determination to carry on regardless. Appropriate change often has to await the emergence of impish difficulties during the period of full implementation. It is the 'imps of implementation' that often bring home to the committed the pragmatic irrationalities of the commitment.

[55] Unlike devils, imps are not intrinsically evil: they are better thought of as mischievous entities whose activities prevent our plans working out as we intended. For an illustrated development of this analogy see Garnett.D (2015), A-Z of Housing (Introduction), London: Palgrave/Macmillan.

[56] In some ways this tendency is analogous to Thomas Kuhn's paradigm psychology in which established science is reluctant to relinquish current theories and practices when confronted with new information, ideas and approaches.

The devil may be in the detail but the imps are in the implementation

When dealing with social policy change, both rational thinking and pragmatism can be overridden by commitment. 'Committed proposals' are likely to be shaped, in part at least, by values and beliefs. When it comes to social issues, reforms are seldom discussed in terms of unadorned logical reasoning. Our attitudes to issues are underpinned by values and the proposals we make for change are then determined by our rationalising attitudes. The fact that so many directives are only modified or abandoned as a result of experiencing difficulties of implementation highlights the tendency of ideological commitment to minimise, or even disregard, the possible (or even probable) negative consequences of changes in policy. Ideologically driven policies also have a tendency to restrict social thinking and planning to narrowly defined, highly particularised goals. In the academic literature it is generally accepted that the pursuit of optimum solutions to complex social problems such as unemployment, crime, homelessness, poor educational attainment, etc., should take account of the fact that sound policies need to seek a multiplicity of interrelated goals and that the use of directives to regulate behaviour can have a multiplicity of consequences.[57] F. Della Croce et al even suggest that when making complex decisions, "there are always different consequences to consider, there are always more objectives and goals to satisfy, there are always more opinions to take into account."[58] This means that policy makers, whether in business or in government, need to understand that "the presence of multiple criteria should be considered the general case, while single criterion optimisation should be considered as a special case."[59]

In business as well as in politics, unanticipated implementation problems are likely to occur when multi-faceted policies that are likely to have multiple consequences are largely discussed in terms of a single criterion.[60] This is the reason for incorporating some form of multiple criteria evaluation into the decision discourse prior to any attempt to formulate an outline policy. This is well understood and when important political or commercial decisions are made that are expected to impose large resource costs or have significant social or environmental consequences, the impacts of the various options will normally be researched and analysed. Although policy makers make extensive use of various forms of cost-benefit and impact analysis, the process of policy formation usually fails to take account of how competing rationalities affect what gets decided. The existence of multiple criteria is usually recognised while the existence of multiple rationalities is usually ignored. The existence of multiple rationalities can lead to ambiguity. Ambiguity can be at the heart of a religious experi-

[57] In the policy-making literature, it is virtually impossible to find any textbook, paper or curriculum that does not make this point.

[58] F. Della Croce, A. Tsoukias and P. Moraitis, (2002) Why is it difficult to make decision under multiple criteria? Paper: American Association for Artificial Intelligence (www.aaai.org).

[59] Ibid.

[60] The following argument also applies to cases of restricted (rather than single) criteria.

ence or an artistic endeavour, but is not normally the sought-for outcome of a technical or social enquiry. Sound science can speculate but such speculation should be grounded in what we already know. In policy formation what is being sought are considerations capable of swaying the intellect.[61]

Note to chapter 3

This chapter can be read as an argument for what I am terming multiple rationality analysis (MRA). It is important to be clear that MRA is not the same thing as multiple criteria analysis (MCA). MCA is one of a number of decision tools that seek to evaluate options by scoring and ranking a range of possible goals. By contrast, MRA sets in place a value context for the decision discourse and then seeks to generate rather than evaluate options. An MRA would precede any evaluation exercise or cost-benefit calculation. MRA is intended to be employed only in instances where there is a degree of ethical uncertainty about what to do. This is why MRA should be seen as relating to moral philosophy rather than economics.

[61] Mill, John Stuart. A System of Logic. New York: Harper & Brothers, 1874.

Ideology

"It is not possible to reason people out of a position that they were not reasoned into in the first place".
(Attributed to Jonathon Swift)

It is difficult to talk or write about the relationship between knowledge, understanding and discourse without confronting the issue of 'ideology'. Most approaches to ideology in the social sciences define it in terms of pejorative notions such as misguided beliefs or false consciousness. Some writers have sought to provide a more penetrating analysis by devising ways of classifying the notion differently with respect to its use in different social science disciplines.[62] For the purposes of the current discussion, however, we will simply use the term 'ideological' when referring to any strongly held belief system that produces intentional bias by drawing contentious inferences that are based on incomplete or selective evidence or depends entirely on non logical reasoning for its justification.

Ideological statements are not consistent with science: they assert claims to truth that are not justified by objective investigation. Stanley Cohen makes the point that a claim to knowledge is its own form of power, "whether or not the knowledge is self deceptive". His point is that ideology serves a purpose other than the simple communication of information – namely the exercise of social control. He describes such claims as "utilitarian forms of knowledge" that act as "alibis" for the exercise of power.[63] Karl Marx made the point that ideology does not so much falsify factual information as misinterpret it so as to distort it in a purposeful way in order to support factional interests.[64]

Ideological argument tends to pattern the discourse by the way it selects, rejects and sequences information and ideas. It is the mechanics of this patterning that rational analysis seeks to make explicit by encouraging the presentation of the full range of ration-

[62] *See for example the work of Teun A. van Dijk.*

[63] *Cohen S (1985), Visions of Social Control, Oxford: Polity Press, pp.29-30.*

[64] *This refers to Marx's critique of bourgeois ideology as expounded in his Theories of Surplus-Value (1863).*

alizations in an openly conscious fashion. This form of discourse analysis's key proposition is that when ideological rationalisations are seen for what they are, they are less likely to constitute a barrier to the emergence of a deep consensus and a robust decision.

REINFORCEMENT

It is not our doubts that divide us but our certainties. It is part of the human condition that while most of us share similar general concerns about the future and how it might impact on our lives, when it comes to what should be done, we can quarrel, squabble and row. In extreme cases, some people are even prepared to maim, mutilate and kill in order to defend their deep-seated ideological beliefs. In the Introduction we made the point that the proposition that many of us are now living in personalised 'information bubbles' in which our entrenched opinions are continuously reinforced and alternative points of view are automatically disparaged, rejected or excluded. The effect of this tendency is to create ideologically insulated polar media worlds where only one set of moral values and instrumental policies are presented and discussed in a positive way.

CONTESTED CONCEPTS

While empiricist and objectivist methodologies seek to set judgement above human interests and values, in the real world of social affairs and public policy formation we have to accept that this is usually not possible and that the best we can do is to arrive at decisions that allow for some sort of workable compromise between various views and interests.[65] The practical objective of multiple rationality analysis is to reconcile particular interests and values through a systematic (but open) deliberative procedure that at an early stage requires each party to the discussion to explain what they understand by the contested concepts that feature in the discourse. These concepts usually carry moral or value charges that play a powerful part in people's arguments. It is therefore sensible, or even essential, that such charged notions used in the decision discourse be openly discussed in the context of the project that is being considered.

[65] The economist Herbert Simon termed this way of making decisions 'satisficing'. Satisficing involves making a reasoned compromise that is 'second best' or 'good enough'. It is important to note that MRA seeks (ideally) something that can stand as a new 'first best'. The new first best becomes the 'pragmatic optimum' rather than a sub-optimal compromise.

Examples of contested concepts that commonly feature in contemporary policy discussions in western democracies include such notions as: 'sustainability', 'efficiency', 'fairness', 'sovereignty', 'diversity', 'equal opportunities', and 'democracy'.

For many people, considering the limits and sources of knowledge will bring to the fore a variety of personal questions associated with religion and politics rather than with traditional academic philosophy. In this chapter we will focus on one of epistemology's primary concerns - namely the credibility of the various sources of knowledge. In chapters 1 and 2 we made the point that the authoritative nature of common sense assertions is powerful because it comes from the world of experience. The idea that genuine knowledge stems from direct experience is compelling: indeed, it is the basis for one of the most influential schools of philosophical thought – empiricism. Empiricists put positive scientific facts above metaphysical speculation. A pure empiricist would contend that, apart from our basic evolutionary reflexes and instinctive reactions, there is no such thing as 'innate knowledge' and that reasoned logic that is devoid of sensory evidence cannot be relied upon to determine truth or inform decisions. In reality, there is no such thing as a pure empiricist. Empiricism is a partial way of thinking not a system of cognition and it is invariably used in conjunction with emotions and subjective thinking. In the real world, experience, evidence, intuition and logic come together in the process of decision-making (see chapter 8).

A pure subjectivist would contend that innate understanding or knowledge that we gain about a subject area by intuition and deduction is superior to any gained by sense experience.[66] Again, in reality, apart from a few congenitally deluded mad people, no one makes important decisions by relying solely on self-authenticating inner perceptions.[67]

[66] One view, generally associated with Descartes, is that what we know a priori is more certain than what we believe on the basis of sense experience: all knowledge acquired through the senses is open to doubt. Another view, generally associated with Plato, locates the superiority of a priori knowledge in the objects known: reason is subject to human fickleness while 'the thing itself' remains what it is (authentic/true).

[67] The relationship between semantics and false conceptions is explored critically by Wilfrid Sellars' famous notion of "the myth of the given" (Wilfrid Sellars – The Stanford Encyclopedia of Philosophy. Metaphysics Research Lab, Stanford University – via Stanford Encyclopedia of Philosophy).

In everyday social and business decision-making, the question is not whether to employ empirical or subjective ways of thinking, but how to bring together evidence and instinctual analysis to gain the knowledge that is necessary to make sustainable decisions.

We have already argued that the danger of relying on common sense as the primary guide to decision-making is that it has a tendency to skew both modes of thinking. When a priori knowledge[68] (in particular that derived from intuition and deduction) is not adequately challenged by evidence, misconceptions (or even delusions) can drive decisions that are later regretted. When a posteriori knowledge (dependant upon sense experience) dominates an argument, other issues may arise. Most obviously, in order to guide decisions, empirical evidence needs to be selected

many hands make light work

and interpreted. To give meaning to the world about us, sensations have to be organised by prior experience and previously acquired knowledge. In the world of social affairs, much evidence is contradictory and there is a tendency for people to favour evidence that supports their established beliefs and ignore evidence that might challenge those beliefs. In any event, facts seldom speak for themselves. The superficiality of common sense assertions is such that they fail to engage with any form of systematic thought: research, objective analysis, or indeed any form of cogent intellectual activity is simply deemed to be unnecessary. Common sense's reliance for validation on experience has one other major weakness highlighted by Gottfried Wilhelm von Leibniz. Over three hundred years ago, he made the point that although knowledge of the exterior world comes to us via our senses, experience alone cannot be relied upon to determine universal realities. He drew attention to the fact that sense experiences are specific to time and place and must therefore be regarded as specific instances rather than general truths. If truth is relative to circumstance then its confirmation requires more than passive observation. To put

[68] Knowledge gained independently of sense experience. The assumption being that our innate knowledge is not learned through either sense experience or intuition and deduction: it is just part of our nature. Deduction is a process in which we derive conclusions from intuited premises through valid arguments - ones in which the conclusion must be true if the premises are true.

it proverbially, it may be reasonable to argue that in a specific instance "too many cooks spoil the broth" but it may also be true that in some other instance, "many hands make light work".[69]

A contemporary of Leibniz, David Hume, considered the distinction between externally derived and internally generated understandings in a way that enabled him to bring more analytical rigour to the debate about the sources of knowledge. Hume began by dividing all mental perceptions between ideas (thoughts) - and impressions (sensations and feelings), and then considered how these two aspects of cognition interrelate to create an understanding of the world. By concluding that complex ideas are derived from sense impressions he established the foundations for subsequent empirical philosophising. One might look to the beginning and end of life to explain Hume's proposition. Babies in the womb, we might surmise, experience physical sensations, but the individual's sophisticated thoughts about the nature of society and the world about us have to await his or her post birth experiences and impressions: our ideas develop as we experience more of the world. Similarly, we might surmise that with death all experience is extinguished and, as a result, all thought processes cease.

By challenging the notion of revelation, Hume's empiricist arguments challenged much of the religious teaching of his day. His reasoning still offers a compelling challenge to those contemporary arguments that enlightened understanding is accomplished through prayer or meditation involving an inward journey to deeper levels of consciousness. Hume's arguments still have currency for writers and thinkers such as Richard Dawkins who argue that knowledge that is not grounded in experience (science) is no more than a "delusion". There is indeed some historical evidence that religious authority or political power that is based on non-scientific assertions is antagonistic to systematic enquiries that might undermine their authority by referencing empirical evidence. As the nineteenth century British statesman John Morley put it, "Where it is a duty to worship the sun, it is pretty sure to be a crime to examine the laws of heat."[70]

[69] To be clear, we are here referring to social understandings. In technical areas such as pure mathematics, there is universal agreement that it is legitimate to assert that the specific instance coincides with the universal truth.

[70] John Morley (1872) Voltaire, London: Chapman and Hall, Second edition, p.14.

Hume's empiricism goes on to postulate that the mental faculties of memory and imagination draw on sense experiences both to interpret the world and to reimagine it. This implies that truly rational understandings of what is and what could be are inevitably rooted in evidence (a posteriori perceptions) rather than beliefs (a priori preconceptions). In this way empiricism can be said to support a pragmatic point of view.

Some recent western thinkers have tended to pursue more of a Cartesian line by maintaining that in addition to what we understand through our senses, there are certain innate ideas and principles that we know independently of experience. Both Descartes and Leibniz had long argued that there exist certain innate principles that we 'know' in a way that is independent of experience. By the twentieth century, writers such Bertrand Russell and Noam Chomsky[71] were arguing that "logical principles are known to us, and cannot by themselves be proved by experience, since all proof presupposes them." (Russell 1912 chapter 7). Such writers remain somewhat diffident about claiming that we are born with knowledge as such, and therefore have tended to avoid using the term "innate" to describe these embedded principles. The claim is that these principles do in fact exist independently of experience although, paradoxically, our awareness of them can only be deduced from experience. It is for this reason that they are usually termed "a priori" rather than "innate".

Because the idea that some forms of knowledge are innate in the sense of being present as such from birth seems implausible, some writers (e.g. Carruthers) maintain that knowledge is only innate in the sense of being innately determined to make its appearance at some later stage in a child's cognitive development.

As Russell puts it, "Thus, while admitting that all knowledge is elicited and caused by experience, we shall nevertheless hold that some knowledge is a priori, in the sense that experience which makes us think of it does not suffice to prove it, but merely so directs our attention that we see its truth without requiring any proof from experience." (The Problems of Philosophy (1912), OUP 1967 edition, p.41).

[71] Chomsky argues that to explain language acquisition, we must assume that learners have an in-built knowledge of a universal grammar capturing the common deep structure of natural languages.

In the highly complex world of social interactions in which we live, not all a priori knowledge is of a strictly logical nature. Although an innate appreciation of mathematical, semantic and logical relationships is clearly knowledge - it does not furnish us with a proper understanding of the external social world. In the world of political, business and social affairs, decisions are informed by another discretely different form of a priori understanding – moral instincts.

FROM MORALS TO ETHICS

Morals are immaterial and as such cannot be perceived through our senses. Modern critical theorists argue that we cannot use moral standards alone to evaluate society because they are self-referential and shaped by the society of which they are a part; therefore they cannot provide a basis for critique: they constitute some sort of code for action rather than an evidence base. However, few would deny that people need some sort of moral code to help them make decisions. Tana French expresses this point by arguing that moral codes are a necessary component of all successful decision-making. "It's not that you do the right thing and hope it pays off; the morally right thing is by definition the thing that gives the biggest payoff."[72]. Social psychologists argue that subscribing to a moral code is not so much driven by material personal interest per se as by a need to conform to the norms of our chosen peer groups – moral acceptance is the price we pay for membership of our socio-cultural communities. In this way, they argue that morality 'blinds and binds' the individual's perceptions. David Hume made this point by arguing that a moral code is a mechanism for judging actions against current standards rather than being an object of universal understanding. He regarded morals as being akin to "taste and sentiment" rather than objects of perception.[73] Ethics might be described as 'morality in action' in that ethical behaviour is seen as behaviour that is informed by a moral code. In this respect, the relationship between morality and ethics might be seen to be analogous to that between science and technology – where technology is seen as 'science in action'. Morality provides a compass pointing to the 'right' direction:

[72] Tana French (2008), In the Woods. London: Penguin Books.

[73] "Beauty, whether moral or natural, is felt more properly than perceived." (Hume 1748, Section XII, Part 3, p. 173).

ethics represent the commitment to take the path pointed to by the compass. In public and business affairs, we might say that ethical awareness is knowing the difference between what you have the right to do and what you believe is right to do. Politicians and corporate leaders who have been criticised for "behaving badly" often react by announcing publicly: "I've done nothing wrong". This can usually be translated as meaning "I knew it was immoral but it wasn't illegal".

To some considerable extent, what is believed to be moral is determined by an individual's predispositions or habitus and therefore what that individual counts as ethical is in part influenced by local (e.g. family, educational or professional) cultural factors. This means that what is regarded to be fair, decent, compassionate or humane is often contested. The question then arises, 'Is ethical behaviour determined solely by cultural factors?' Are there any universal human values that remain constant over time and between cultures? The issue as to whether there exist cross-cultural values that are recognised through time remains a live question in philosophy and politics. It is one of those questions that evades a definitive resolution. Arguably, the opposing poles of the philosophical argument are represented by Immanuel Kant's notion of the categorical imperative on one side and existentialist thinking on the other.

The Kantian position

Writing at a time when scientific progress was rapid and apparent,[74] Kant, like other thinkers of his day, confronted the fundamental question underlying modern analytical philosophy, namely - 'What is the nature of reason?' Kant argued that only by addressing this question can we determine the nature of morality and say anything meaningful about ethical behaviour. He would

a "categorical imperative"

have regarded pragmatic arguments for ethical behaviour (such as Rousseau's idea of the 'social contract' or Bentham's utilitarianism) as socially understandable but philosophically superficial and therefore ultimately unsound.

[74] Subsequently referred to rather loosely as 'The Age of Reason'.

Because it is not possible to validate any assumed congruence of sense perceptions of external objects with the essential nature of such objects, Kant argued that it is not possible to equate the 'out there' independent reality with our 'in-our-heads' experiences of it. From this he argued that the inconstant nature of reason means that it is not possible to understand reality by its use alone. More specifically, he made the point that pragmatic explanations of ethical behaviour all too often lead to contradictions and some sort of impasse and therefore pragmatic reasoning cannot be trusted to reflect reality.

According to Kant, morality is an embedded aspect of the human condition: it is not so much a product of reason as an over-arching imperative commanding reason. He saw it as an internally structured precondition of being human. He linked morality to ethics by defining a 'moral imperative' as a proposition that asserts the necessity for taking (or not taking) a certain action. For Kant, such qualities as intelligence, talent, security, perseverance and pleasure can be judged to be 'worthy' and can be sought after or admired, but they cannot be regarded as 'moral' conditions as such. For Kant a moral act is a matter of duty – a duty to follow what is intrinsically good. For Kant, this 'duty' has an absolute quality (is a "categorical imperative") and is distinguished from any voluntaristic obligation (such as a contractual obligation).

To be genuinely 'moral' Kant argued that a position must be "good without qualification". A condition such as 'happiness' cannot be regarded as good in itself because if cruel or criminal acts give you pleasure, the drive for your happiness could lead to a situation that others might reasonably regard as ethically unacceptable. The Kantian conclusion is that the only thing that can be regarded as 'good' without any conceivable qualification is an individual's "will" to do the right thing. In this context the word "will" carries complex connotations about the nature of being human that has engaged much philosophical thought including that of St. Augustine, Schopenhauer, Hume and Nietzsche. Such thinkers pointed to the idea that all the external manifestations of a human being are embedded in a non-observable, context-free, internal, fundamental state of inner being - or "will" - that acts as the master rather than the servant of the intellect. This conception of the categorical imperative argues that an act can only be regarded as truly ethical if it is derived from a fundamental moral tenet that the actor wills to be a universal law.

Only actions that are guided by this deep-seated motivation to do the right thing can be regarded as truly moral: doing the 'right thing' for pragmatic reasons does not count. That an action conforms to the precepts of an individual's inner beliefs about what constitutes honesty, compassion, fairness, etc., is not in itself enough to qualify it as moral behaviour: it must be motivated by a "duty" to commit to the inner will to act for the good: it is deep-seated motivations not good consequences that count. The moral person does not simply 'do good' but acts in accordance with his or her "will" to do good. If a point of view or action is motivated by self-interest or delusion it cannot by classed as moral.[75] From the eighteen century onwards, this Kantian argument has been used as a starting point for a wide range of philosophical arguments about the place of religious and political beliefs in the 'good society'.

THE EXISTENTIALIST POSITION

An implication of the natural rationalist (neo-Kantian) position is that experience can trigger our awareness of moral knowledge, but it does not furnish us with it – it pre-exists as part of the human condition. Existentialist thinkers treat discussions about the nature and scope of ethical behaviour differently. Rather than pointing to a fixed Kantian imperative as the basis for ethical behaviour, writers such as Søren Kierkegaard, Jean Paul Sartre and Simone de Beauvoir argued that we make and adapt our personal morality as we live and grow. In this way, moral positions emerge as we rationalise our experiences of the world: our attitudes towards what counts as right or wrong grows and shifts as we construct a path through life. The argument here is that the full content of any commitment to a moral position only unfolds itself as we engage with it. As rational beings, we should remain open to the possibility that in the future we will see and judge things in a different way than we do now.

[75] In the twentieth century, much of this philosophical analysis gets recast in the methods and language of psychology.

The existentialist position is clearly open to the proposition that moral beliefs are culturally determined. Cultural historians have described, and in some cases analysed, how moral conformity is created and continually transformed within particular communities. These historical works focus on how collective, institutionalised behaviour emerges and constantly changes within cultural settings. In his studies of sexuality and crime Michel Foucault, for example, sought to demonstrate that notions such as 'deviance' and 'punishment' are defined by society and do not occur "naturally". Arguably, how the state treats its citizens and how citizens behave towards each other defines the nature of an age. Together with its landmark artistic and technological achievements, a society is defined by its 'zeitgeist'.[76]

More tentatively, it might also be argued that history points to the existence of some form of constant inter-cultural morality. This suggestion rests on a neo-Kantian view that periodic barbarism (and lesser forms of repression) stems from the emergence of power interests and dysfunctional political arrangements rather than from personal deep-seated innate knowledge of 'good and evil'. This thesis would assume, for example, that the genocidal regimes of Genghis Khan, Mary Tudor, Adolf Hitler, Mao Zedong and Pol Pot should be seen, when taking the long view, as historical aberrations. The argument here is that their very notoriety makes them 'examples that prove the rule'; that is, the rule that we have, and always have had, a priori moral knowledge of what is 'right' and what is 'wrong' and that even at the time when the repressions were being enacted, those who were perpetrating the exploitive acts or experiencing the consequences of those acts, understood them to be 'wrong' at some deep level of understanding.

If historians are able to identify an inter-cultural moral consensus within a particular community and describe the consequential societal behaviours that stem from this, it would seem to suggest the probable existence through time and space of some form of recurring inter-cultural agreement about the boundaries of ethical behaviour. This brings us back to the question as to whether or not

[76] The existence of 'zeitgeist' is controversial. It is however commonly used to describe attitudes that are currently 'in the air'.

it is reasonable to postulate that there exists some form of universal morality that holds independently of context or culture. To some considerable extent, this question hinges on the existence or otherwise of 'natural law' – a long-standing debate that has been at the intellectual centre of philosophical arguments since the Enlightenment. Michel de Montaigne for example, pointed to inconsistencies in "laws of conscience" (moral beliefs) that clearly stem from local customs rather than from some form of universal ethic. That is, they are grounded in human culture(s) rather than God-given truths.[77] In arguing the case for his particular form of relativistic thinking, Richard Rorty argues that we should more readily accept philosophy's association with modern Darwinian pragmatism and focus on the relationship between our drives to survive and our notions of morality. In facing up to this practical reality about the human condition, he implies that we could simplify the argument and be free from the fruitless search for unconditional, transcultural moral obligations that are assumed to be rooted in an unchanging ahistorical human nature.[78] We will explore this pragmatic point of view more fully in the next chapter. Before we do, it is worth pointing to the existence of the United Nations as an institution and the Universal Declaration of Human Rights as an adopted international code. This does indicate that in our own time, there exists some degree of agreement about what constitutes basic human values and acceptable political behaviour within and between national and cultural boundaries.[79]

Business Ethics

Phronēsis (from the Ancient Greek φρόνησις) is a term used in philosophy to describe a type of practical intelligence. In particular, it refers to the type of wisdom employed in the pursuit of specific goals. It is a notion derived from Aristotle who used it to distinguish practical intelligence from other forms of wisdom. In particular, he used the term to distinguish the capability to think rationally in particular situations from reasoning that is based on

[77] For further discussion of this aspect of Enlightenment see Pagden A. (2013), The Enlightenment and Why it Still Matters. Oxford: OUP pp. 44-46.

[78] Rorty R. (1999) Introduction, p.xvi.

[79] We might also argue that the emergence of common values through time and between cultures is witnessed by the commentaries and judgements of generations of critics whose opinions about the works of Da Vinci, Utamaro, Beethoven, Shakespeare, Dostoyevsky, etc. accumulate to provide a lasting inter-cultural consensus about artistic value.

universal truths (sophia). For Aristotle, the practice of phronēsis requires political nous as well as the ability to reason cogently. Perhaps unsurprisingly, the contemporary debate about the nature of 'business ethics' does not make much reference to the long-standing concerns of the foundational philosophers referred to in this chapter. Although ethics is now a major topic within business education, the works of Immanuel Kant and Jean Paul Sartre do not feature strongly in the curricula of business schools. The intellectual foundations of business ethics tend to have a pragmatic rather than a philosophical focus. Theoretical analysis in this area looks more to the disciplines of welfare economics, psychology and sociology than it does to academic philosophy when trying to link the notions of ethics and practical intelligence.

Successful businesses are inevitably goal orientated and those regarded as 'successful' business people tend to display skill clusters that form the basis of their abilities to think rationally and behave politically in particular situations. Over the years there has been a great deal of sociological analysis of political motivations. Drawing on Aristotle's classical distinction between the universal and the specific, Max Weber argued that political conduct can be orientated within either an 'ethic of responsibility' (Verantwortungsethik) or an 'ethic of ultimate ends' (Gesinnungsethik). Relating this to the business environment, and translating it into a more common parlance, we might say that ethical business practices embrace the pursuit of both 'means and ends'. Many commercial organisations render this ethical dualism in contemporary management jargon by making public statements about their "values and mission".

An interesting (and significant) aspect of contemporary discussions about the nature and scope of business ethics centres on whether the drive for both ethical outcomes (e.g. social and environmental improvements) together with the pursuit of proprietary interests (e.g. profits and share values) should be regarded as a dualism or a duality. This debate is currently being given a focus by the emerging idea of 'shared value' that argues that society as a whole (not just shareholders) has a 'stake' in what businesses do.[80]

[80] See Appendix 1 for an explanation of 'shared value'.

Steve Denning has made the point[81] that we can no longer simply embrace the "greed is good" philosophy of Michael Douglas's character in the 1987 film Wall Street. Indeed the fact that this ironic film was produced at all indicates that by the 1980s there was a significant change of mood about business attitudes in society at large. This change in mood provides an opportunity to create a different type of business culture that is fit for purpose in the twenty first century. The emerging shift in business ethics is being scrutinised by a number of business schools - notably Harvard that has termed the new approach "shared value". Harvard's empirical research indicates that in the twenty first century, the creation and sharing of value will be seen as the key to both political and corporate success. Many modern management analysts now argue that ethical behaviour is seen to be both morally 'right' and the pragmatic thing to do: it is quite simply 'best practice'.

[81] Forbes Leadership, February 22 2012

Warranted Assertions

"New opinions are always suspected and usually opposed without any other reason but because they are not already common."
(John Locke)

Although empiricists argue that the credibility of a belief should be commensurate with the reliability of the source, sometimes for some people, no matter what the source, empirical evidence can be less persuasive than religious revelation, political commitment or traditional habits. The 'credibility problem' is no less of an issue today than it was at the time of Locke.

In the modern popular understanding of how to validate what is right, something is regarded as 'true' if it corresponds to the 'facts' and/or is coherent in the sense that it is logically consistent with currently accepted ways of determining what is correct. If a statement fails to reflect our current understanding of reality or contradicts other propositions that are already accepted as being true, then there is a prima facie case against its veracity.

The notions of correspondence and coherence are, to some extent at least, culturally determined rather than independent absolutes. In many instances practical policy discussions lack coherence because of competing personal or group priorities. Successful interagency working, for example, requires the coming together of different professional cultures to solve complex social problems. The recent growth of interagency working is being intensified by the rapid introduction of the 'joint commissioning' model of service provision. Local government officers, councillors, civil servants, private sector service providers and facilitating consultants are important players in this field. These 'expert groups' will doubtless hold differing views about what 'best' to do. Internal tensions and differences of opinion can also arise between individuals or teams within a single organisation. Competing priorities can also occur because a policy will have an impact on a variety of external (non-proprietary) interests that are different from those of the investing agency responsible for the decision. If these different or wider stakeholder perceptions and interests are not taken into account at the outset, final policy decisions are likely to be unstable because affected parties are likely to argue that the new policy is unreasonable, unfair or in some other respect unacceptable.

For those embedded in their own self-interests, it can be difficult to accept that other concerns are legitimate and should be taken into consideration when making social policy decisions. Where analysis is limited and arguments are founded on a restricted range of rationalities, what counts as the right action can be felt to be self-evident and not open to compromise. For some who hold uncompromising beliefs or have a strong pecuniary or other pragmatic interest in the outcome of a decision, determining what should be done is, for them, unproblematic and as easy as finding an elephant in a haystack.

In this chapter we will consider how the world looks from the point of view of a pragmatist. In so doing we will encounter some of the ideas of the so-called "Father of Pragmatism" C.S. Pierce (1839-1914). Pierce regarded a belief as a habitualized rule for action. In so doing, he sought to disassociate the notion from the traditional Cartesian assumption that a belief statement is the end result of the mind's search for an unencumbered objective truth. Pragmatists like Pierce shifted the debate about the nature of belief away from the field of pure reason towards that of down-to-earth Darwinian logic. This pragmatic way of seeing things treats a belief as a sort of practical tool that is available to further the interests of individuals. In other words, beliefs are thought statements that are used by people to help them cope: cope that is, with both the complex (and sometimes dangerous) external world of social relationships and the fraught internal world of moral uncertainties and ethical dilemmas.

PRAGMATIC TRUTH

The notion of 'pragmatic truth' emerged from the works of nineteenth century thinkers such as Charles Pierce who argued that our beliefs underpin what we do by providing our lives with 'rules for action'. Pierce argued that to give meaning to a proposition we need to understand its practical implications: this idea became known as "the pragmatism principle".[82]

[82] Published as an article titled 'How to Make our Ideas Clear' in Popular Science Monthly, January 1879, vol.vii.

We might say that before the emergence of pragmatic philosophy, post Enlightenment thinking tended to regard 'truth' as an objective reality independent of our perceptions of reality. This meant that much philosophical energy was expended on trying to understand and reconcile the gap that was assumed to exist between 'what seems to be' and 'what actually is'. The extreme case of this philosophical anxiety about the reality gap was expressed by Descartes's well-known concerns that we can be sure of nothing except that we are thinking. Pragmatist philosophers sidestepped these thoughts, seeing them as unnecessarily negative and fruitlessly intellectual.

In 1907 William James expanded the pragmatism principle in a series of lectures dedicated to the memory of John Stuart Mill.[83] This lecture series might be said to mark the point at which philosophers began to argue in a systematic way that in the social world of practical affairs, truth might be thought of as a relative rather than an absolute phenomenon.

Some would argue that it was Emmanuel Kant who first questioned the possibility of philosophy matching our concepts with the objective world 'out there' beyond perception. In bringing into question whether independent reality could ever be fully accessible to human conception, he established the idea that philosophy might have to make do with a 'sufficiency' of understanding. In some ways, his distinction between the noumenal (real) and phenomenal (perceptible by the senses) worlds opened the door for pragmatism to enter the debate about the meaning of truth.

If truth can be conceived as 'what works' (or "what it is useful to believe" as James put it), then a case might be made for saying that what is true for one person may not be true for someone else. Some modern writers[84] have extended James's ideas by arguing that our understanding of truth and right action has to be put into a Darwinian context. The argument here is that pragmatism is an embedded aspect of evolution and because we are evolved creatures, we are instinctively motivated to search for the 'truth' only in so far as it is useful. In other words, evolution predisposes

[83] The series was given at Harvard University and was entitled 'Pragmatism: A New Name to Old Ways of Thinking' and is republished as a free book on line by www.Gutenberg.org (2013)

[84] See for example John Gray (2015) The Soul of the Marionette: A Short Enquiry In Human Freedom. Also Evolution and Social Psychology (2006), Eds. Mark Shaller et.al.

us to pursue what works in our interest rather than some notion of absolute truth.

Relative truth

In the world of social affairs, claims to truth are seldom absolute. Indeed, by using the term 'claims to truth' we are indicating that in this sort of analysis, an assumption is being made that social truth is a relative notion (what I understand to be) rather than an absolute fact (what is). Although this particular take on the nature of truth does not reject the significance of coherence and correspondence reasoning, it also consciously incorporates questions of human interests into the analysis.

The idea of a 'macro-discourse'

In practice, policy formulations and resource decisions are made in the context of some form of wider social interaction that we are here terming a macro-discourse. This wider notion of discourse is derived from an established academic literature (notably the writings of critical theorists such as Jurgen Habermas, Michel Foucault and Peter Berger) that postulate that meanings and social understandings are embodied in current operational processes, institutional procedures, social conventions, pedagogic practices, editorial arrangements, etc. In this way, we can say, for example, that those members of a community who are studying, teaching, managing, researching or campaigning for educational change, etc., at a particular time and place are, by virtue of their interactions, engaging in that society's current education macro-discourse. Similarly the complex of interactions between politicians, police officers, journalists, judges, court officials, researchers, professional and lay commentators, etc. together determine the nature and scope of a society's current macro-discourse on criminal justice. Within such a mega perception, any institutional practice through which the social production of meaning takes place is considered to be part of the macro-discourse.

This particular understanding of discourse, and discourse analysis, draws heavily on Michel Foucault's ideas on the matter. Foucault understands discourses as expressions of power/knowledge-relations. Discourse in the Foucauldian sense is less about everyday linguistic interaction ('micro-discourse'), and more about historically located systems of ideas that form institutionalized and authoritative ways of addressing a topic. Discourse in this sense does not only shape our particular ways of talking about a subject matter, it also constitutes our understanding of what is normal, natural, and true. Thus, both subjective and objective reality are constituted, constructed, and maintained through the particular macro-discourses available in any given epoch.

The notion that at different times there exists some kind of unspoken and unconscious overarching field of understanding providing the boundaries of acceptable knowledge is a recurring theme in philosophical thought. Borrowing a term from early nineteenth century German philosophy, modern popular writers often talk of the zeitgeist - meaning 'the spirit of the age'. In The Order of Things (1970), Foucault introduced the more specific idea of an episteme which can be thought of as a set of anonymous, ordered, unconscious, historical rules and codes that constitute the cultural foundation (a form of 'historical a priori') for determining what gets regarded as being accepted knowledge in a particular period and for a given social, economic, geographical or linguistic area (such as Renaissance Italy or Britain during the 'Industrial Revolution'). Critics of Foucault regard the notion as 'difficult' to pin down – particularly as Foucault himself seems to have used it differently at different times. We might simply think of it as a kind of unspoken and unconscious 'stratum' of assumptions that provide the cultural preconditions for accepted knowledge in each historical period. By using the term 'stratum' we can reflect Foucault's thought that to unearth the episteme of a period we have to engage in a metaphorical cultural 'archaeology'. Each episteme from one period to the next is supposed to be discontinuous and incommensurable in the sense of being radically different and in any given culture and at any given moment there is always only one episteme that defines the conditions of possibility of all knowledge - whether expressed in a theory or silently embedded in a practice.[85] In the Anglo-American philosophical vocabulary, the notion of episteme has much in common with Thomas Kuhn's idea of a scientific paradigm or conceptual framework. A scientific

[85] For further reading on this aspect of Foucault's thinking see: Michel Foucault (1970), The Order of Things, An Archaeology of the Human Sciences, London: Tavistock Publications; Clare O'Farrell (1989), Foucault: Historian or Philosopher? Basingstoke: Mcmillan; and J.G Merquior (1985), Foucault, London: Fontana, chapter 3.

paradigm is thought of as a 'disciplinary matrix' that constitutes the tradition within which the inquirer is operating. In this way, Kuhn argues that even the natural sciences have to be seen as practices that are founded on sets of beliefs relative to certain cultures or sub-cultures.

ABSOLUTE TRUTH

Foucault's line of thought leads us to take a relativistic approach to discourse analysis - 'truth is relative to discourse'. The place of forensic truth in social affairs is limited to evidence (often statistical) that can be called upon to challenge or support a discursive argument. The point to be made is that in social affairs (and policy making in general) the pursuit of absolute truth is illusory and is best abandoned for the search for considered best practice. To borrow a phrase from Albie Sachs, we are here considering "the truth of experience"[86] that can be regarded as a type of reality that is established by sharing our experiences in interaction, discussion and debate.[87]

It is sometimes the case that in policy debates a protagonist will seek to hold onto a rigid position by referencing some absolutist value that they present as a fundamental 'principle' that they are not prepared to relinquish. These notions of universal social truths and principled positions take us into complex philosophical territory that is explored in some detail in later chapters. Here we will simply suggest that sustainable policy agreements are best pursued by making 'warranted assertions' rather than by pointing to some assumed universal truth.

WARRANTED ASSERTIONS

For some, the idea that there can be a plurality of rationalities and that in the field of social affairs 'truth' is related to interests and relative to discourse, are uncomfortable notions. In particular, they present potential problems for social campaigners and politicians seeking clear, unambiguous programmes of reform. The practical problems that stem from the relative nature of 'social truth' were addressed in the early decades of the twentieth

[86] Jurist on the South African Truth and Reconciliation Commission.

[87] In the management literature, the 'truth of experience' is sometimes referred to as 'the truth of requisite variety'.

century by the American academic and social thinker John Dewey. Dewey was schooled in the pragmatist tradition and thought that social enquiry should focus on real-life problems such as curing disease, reducing crime or improving living conditions, rather than on the more arcane issue of refining our underlying philosophical beliefs. He was both an educationalist and an active social reformer. He advocated that social enquiry should be a spur to social change and that policies should be informed by evidence that was gathered and analysed by sound research methods. He argued that the key purpose of this form of pragmatic enquiry should be to improve people's lives.

Dewey's pragmatism included an evolutionary view of social research. He not only believed that over time competent social investigations would uncover new facts that would enable us to build on past understandings of the needs of society, but also that the methods of enquiry themselves will evolve and become more effective. This form of scientific optimism led him to develop the notion of "warranted assertions". For a proposition to be "warranted" in Dewey's sense, it has to be backed up by skilled research that produces sufficient evidence to assert it as true to the best of our knowledge.[88] In this way, the pragmatic approach to policy formation and decision-making involves creating and assessing options with a view to agreeing a programme that will improve people's lives. The best outcome is not only based on a proper appraisal of options, but also on an assumption that the right options are being appraised. In many instances this not a dilemma and does not present a problem.

In some decision-making situations the need for rigorous argument over key choices may not be necessary (as in the case of a sole trader deciding to replenish her stock or a police officer deciding to arrest a criminal 'caught in the act'). Also, no dilemma exists where there is no disagreement about what constitutes best practice. However, in many areas of commercial, social and political life a choice/agreement dilemma features strongly in the decision discourse.

[88] This approach can lead to a somewhat circular argument that 'knowledge' is simply the output of competent enquiry and that 'truth' is simply what competent enquiry deems it to be.

In seeking a deep-seated agreement that is 'sustainable' in the sense in which we are using the term (see Introduction), systematic account has to be taken of how warranted proposals impact on the interests of all those who have some current or future stake in the outcome. This points to the need to broaden the notion of 'stakeholders' so that decision-makers become widely accountable for the options they generate, appraise and implement.[89] Only in this way can the claim be made that the final decision warrants support.

The choice/agreement dilemma is prominent in the world of public affairs. In this area of decision-making, it is generally recognised that local councils, schools, health agencies, the police, housing associations, etc. should engage a variety of interest groups in discussions about how a particular organisation can make the best use of its limited resources. The recognition of this point of view is witnessed by the now common reference to "stakeholders" in both official policy documents and the academic social policy literature. Indeed, it is now such a ubiquitous concept that 'stakeholder analysis' is a project management tool in common use by a wide variety of agencies.[90]

Working with a number of leading companies, Harvard Business School has extended the notion of 'stakeholder interest' in an attempt to devise an approach to business that is appropriate for the twenty-first century. Broadly speaking, the argument is that subsequent to the financial crisis of the 1980s, the single-minded pursuit of shareholder interests has become unacceptable and successful businesses in the future must both be seen by others and see themselves as contributing to the welfare of the wider community. For the twenty-first century company, being part of the community is more than a public relations exercise - it is a prerequisite for success. See in particular the work of M.E. Porter and M.R. Kramer on the notion of "shared value" which is discussed in Appendix 1.

DISTORTED COMMUNICATION

Examining the mechanics of the decision discourse takes us into language philosophy - particularly the ideas of writers such

[89] That is, accountable to all appropriate stakeholders, including the poor and inarticulate and future as well as present, citizens.

[90] The idea of an individual or group having a stake in a decision emphasizes (or at least implies) that they have some material interest in what happens rather than that they have moral concerns.

as Jurgen Habermas and Basil Bernstein.[91] Through the use of case studies, researchers in this field have looked at how decision discussions about what to do for the best get "distorted" by a lack of understanding between people about each other's underlying (often hidden) rationalities.[92] To put the argument simply, we can say that to achieve true consensus requires undistorted discussion in which people explain the rationalisations underpinning their propositions, suggestions and assertions. To the old saying, "assertion is not proof", we might add "proclamation is not consensus" and, more significantly, "imposed policies are not sustainable".

If a government minister asserts, for example, that "it is only right that social tenants should be allowed to purchase their rented homes at a discounted price", I may agree or disagree – there is clearly a hidden value discourse behind the assertion. Maybe the underlying argument is that having paid rent for a period, the tenant is entitled to a discount.....or maybe it is that for most people, home ownership is a normal and desirable form of tenure and should therefore be encouraged...... Whatever it is, the hidden discourse needs to be exposed and incorporated into the argument if we are seeking a lasting consensus about the tenants' "right to buy".[93] All need to agree, not simply that the proposal is workable, but also with the minister's underlying rationale that the desire for home ownership is in some way "natural" or "worthy" and therefore warranted.

The use of multiple rationality analysis as a pragmatic practice is based on the proposition that: ***if people are debating a complex issue in an open and intelligent fashion and are all genuinely seeking a consensus that will allow them to make a sustainable decision, they need to understand each other's underlying (and often undeclared) attitudes, values and preconceptions.***

For you and me to participate in an undistorted discourse (i.e. what language philosophers refer to as an 'ideal speech' situation), I need to understand not only what you think, but also why you

[91] Such writers have sought to apply the influential philosophical work on language use by writers such as John Searle to social and political settings.

[92] For a development of this idea, see Habermas's writings on "distorted communication".

[93] See Garnett D. and Perry J. (2005), Housing Finance, Coventry: Chartered Institute of Housing, (chapter 6) for a fuller exposition of this example.

think what you think and you need to understand why I think what I think. From this inter-subjective understanding and exposure of our beliefs and values, we can work more effectively together towards some sort of consensus about what should be done for the best. If a consensus is arrived at by such an open mechanism, we might regard the conclusion as "deep" and "sustainable". By contrast, we should regard a policy decision arrived at by a competitive process of partially reasoned assertions as "surface" and "temporary". In practical policy-making, people often behave as protagonists and as such they debate in generalisations and make unsubstantiated assertions - but to produce sustainable outcomes, generalisations have to be worked for. Assertions have to be justified and the justifications have to be understood rather than simply asserted. In this spirit of reasoned optimism, we will explore this proposition in more depth in the following chapters.

Generative vs Competitive Discourse

"Most quarrels amplify a misunderstanding."
(Andre Gide)

It was the Italian poet and man of letters Cesare Pavese who observed that "mistakes are always initial".[94] Draftsmen will tell you that small errors at the beginning of a task become magnified as the task progresses. This is true whether that which is being drafted is a mathematical equation, a technical drawing or a social policy. As we have seen, pragmatists seek to avoid major policy mistakes by making sure that, to the best of their ability, their starting assumptions and propositions are not only rational but also "warranted".

Truth claims about social policy-making can only be accepted as warranted through deliberation. In most policy areas there are no scientifically 'truthful' answers to problems raised - the best that can be hoped for is some deepening of the level of 'consensus'.

Note:
The notion of 'consensus' can be misleading. It is sometimes used in political debate to indicate a situation in which differences or divisions of opinion are avoided or evaded by agreeing to move to some central ground that is not completely comfortable to either party. In other words, the notion of 'consensus' can apply to some form of reluctant 'concession' rather than a genuine inter-subjective agreement. It is for this reason that in this essay we will substitute the word 'agreement' for that of 'consensus'.

In this chapter we will consider the distinction between an agreement arrived at through competitive argument and one that is generated through inter-subjective understanding.

Science and technology may contribute to the argument about where best to site a new waste recycling plant, whether to legalise

[94] W. H. Auden and Louis Kronenberger (1962), The Faber Book of Aphorisms, London & Boston: Faber, p.58.

the recreational use of cannabis, or whether to fell some ancient trees to widen a dangerous stretch of road, but they cannot be relied upon to provide incontrovertible proof of what constitutes the 'correct' course of action. It is for this reason that when analysing multiple rationalities, the pursuit of truth is eclipsed by the more pragmatic goal of a deeper understanding about what constitutes the most appropriate option. In our formulation, the notion of proof is replaced by the notion of warranted justification. The proposition is that this will produce a policy proposal that is more 'sustainable' (less likely to be regretted) than one that was achieved through competitive argument.[95] The methodology being advocated is one that employs considered thought in open discussion. The hoped-for outcome is to replace a reluctant compromise with a positive inter-subjectively understood agreement achieved by substituting a competitive discourse with one that can be described as "generative".

Knowing that and knowing how

In his 1987 book, The Art of the Deal, Donald Trump described his days as being stuffed with meetings and phone calls. Some 30 years later, as President, he still constantly interacted with other people - at rallies, in interviews and press conferences and, most famously, on social media. Commenting on his own ability to transfer insights gained as a businessman into the field of politics, he said:

> *"Many of our problems, caused by years of stupid decisions, or no decisions at all, have grown into a huge mess. If I could wave a magic wand and fix them, I'd do it. But there are a lot of different voices – and interests – that have to be considered when working towards solutions. This involves getting people into a room and negotiating compromises until everyone walks out of that room on the same page."*
> (Dan P McAdams The Atlantic, June 2016 edition "Politics" https://www.theatlantic.com/magazine/archive/2016/06/the-mind-of-donald-trump/480771/)

In a democratic setting, when confronting complex problems that require difficult decisions, we need to come to some sort

[95] This is a rather tautologous point as we are defining this 'deeper' agreement as one that is not regretted in the long run.

of agreement. The tricky thing is, however, deciding how to go about achieving such an agreement. Donald Trump's approach has been wholeheartedly competitive. In his advice to business executives and other dealmakers, he argues the case for "thinking big", "fighting" and "using your leverage". His approach has always been distinctly non-collaborative. "I aim high and then I just keep pushing and pushing to get what I'm after".[96]

Trump's attitude is an extreme example (perhaps the definitive case) of the competitive attitude to deal making and it has to be understood that it really is a 'personal attitude' rather than a 'considered strategy'. When negotiating he is everywhere and at all times combative. He does not so much operate a competitive tactic as have a competitive mind-set. Psychologists describe this phenomenon as operating within a 'personal schema'. A schema is an embedded psychological structure or attitude of mind that provides the individual with a safe and familiar cognitive framework for interacting with others when discussing complex decisions. A fixed mind-set narrows a person's focus to a limited number of familiar ways of engaging in argument. A strong personal schema might result from psychological insecurity around questions of identity. In extreme cases it can be the result of persistent religious or political indoctrination or from what psychiatrists call a personality defect (such as 'malignant narcissism'). A lack of awareness about one's own schemata may imprison a person in an inescapable mind-set. Complex decisions are simplified by tunnel vision - but narrowly framed thinking is unlikely to result in sustainable outcomes. A tunnel takes you in one direction and hides from view everything but a predetermined destination.

The competitive mind-set

Competition is the key characteristic of market theory. Economists have attempted to deal with the question of market compromise through what is termed the theory of second best. Where the desired outcome of 'sustainability' involves compromise, the individual may regard what is being proposed as a 'second best' result from the point of view of his or her initial assumptions about where to go and how best to get there. Desired outcomes are only

[96] When Trump was a child, his father encouraged him to be a "killer" and channel his natural aggression into real estate business dealings. (Robert Maass/Corbis).

subjective models but the single-minded pursuit of what "I want" is often unrealistic in the real world. In the end we may agree to abandon our initial preconception of what is needed and go along with something similar or – more surprisingly – something quite different. We may go along with the different suggestion for pragmatic reasons, abandoning an insistence upon adopting what we began by thinking in the interests of something that will 'work'.

Kelvin Lancaster and Richard G. Lipsey, in their influential article The General Theory of Second Best (1956)[97], considered the problem of what to do when some or all of the necessary conditions to achieve a desired 'best outcome' do not exist. The main idea in this article was that when a constraint prevents the fulfilment of one of these conditions, some or all of the other conditions may then no longer be pertinent. An altogether new optimum situation might then be sought that abandons previously sought-after conditions. This new optimum they called "second best". This way of thinking takes us back to one of our underlying propositions – namely that in business and politics the pursuit of 'truth' should be subordinated to the pursuit of 'best practice'. Put another way, we might say that sustainable decisions cannot just be visionary – they also have to be pragmatic. To say that sound decisions emerge from the rational interplay between theoretical visions and empirical realities based on knowledge is so obvious that we might regard it to be axiomatic. Because it is such a non-contentious point, it can sometimes provide a positive starting point of agreement for those locked into what appears to be a fundamental disagreement about what constitutes 'best practice'.

Knowledgeable actors and experts

Following the conventions of established critical theory, we are referring to the decision-makers as 'actors'. This helps to emphasise the point that a discourse is more than a simple language event.[98] Following the logic of structuration theory, we are assuming that those engaged in decision-making are "knowledgeable actors" in a particular sense: that is, they have a subtle form of practical consciousness that comes into play when they engage in discursive

[97] Building on ideas from an earlier work by James E. Meade.

[98] The proposition that actions are aspects of discourse is discussed fully in the Introduction.

activities. The notion of knowledgeability is different in kind from both general knowledge and specialised expertise.

Human knowledge and cultural evolution
Outside of human cognition, knowledge can be thought of as information that has causal power. In other words, knowledge is the information needed to facilitate change (like the information embedded in DNA). This form of coded knowledge enables things (including the reproduction of life itself) to happen. When knowledge is embraced by human cognition its effects extend beyond the simple causal – it then not only allows change to occur, but in addition, it carries the power to analyse and make judgements about what changes should take place when, where and how. It is this wider explanatory knowledge that lies at the heart of critical theory and constitutes what we mean by 'human knowledge' in these essays.

In its usual definition, 'human knowledge' refers to the results of education or, more generally, to the acquisition of useful or interesting information. An 'expert' possesses 'know-how' as well as 'know-what': normally he or she is regarded as someone who not only possesses a high level of specialised information but is also proficient in certain skill sets. There is a limit to the scope of expertise. If this were not the case, economists would all agree with each other about how to create wealth, there would be no ethical dilemmas or clinical disagreements in medicine, and financial experts would be buying stock not selling advice. Having said this, in many instances it would make good sense for scientists, qualified professionals and other 'experts' with specialised knowledge to join the process of deliberation in order to guide and inform the lay decision-making actors and their stakeholders in order to help them determine what constitutes a 'warranted decision'.

Structuration theory argues that participants in a discourse have the capacity to understand their own and others' values, attitudes and interests and that this facility can affect how they engage with each other. The argument is that this innate cognitive ability enables actors to develop a degree of inter-subjective understanding of what is being discussed. This in turn liberates the individual from the constraints imposed by self-centred schemata and tunnel vision. This is significant because it can expedite a shift towards a more generative mode of interacting. The key point being that such a shift brings about a shared awareness of the importance of creating as well as appraising options. It is in this way that the 'second best' is no longer regarded as a compromise but as a newly conceived 'first best'. In the absence of this cognitive shift, an agreement can be competitively negotiated, while failing to be inter-subjectively accepted. This leads to a decision that is intrinsically unstable. A successful competitive discourse always produces a surface-level compromised 'second best' outcome. By contrast, a successful generative discourse produces a deeper inter-subjective appreciation of what should be done. An agreed 'first best' decision arrived at through generative discourse is more likely to produce a sustainable outcome.

Competitive Discourse and the Appraisal of Options

Negotiation and fought-for compromises are the key features of a competitive discourse. Those involved seek to manage the decision-making process in ways that will advance their own proposal(s) and provide an effective challenge to those opposing views being put forward by others. If initially they fail to achieve everything they want, they will usually move to negotiate a compromise. The Christian evangelist Joyce Meyer put it well when she said that to compromise simply means that you go a "little bit below" what you wanted at the start.[99] In this competitive way of thinking, a negotiated settlement is a process of incremental compromises. Competitive debate is always in danger of being manipulated by particular individuals who are concerned to ensure that what gets accepted is in line with their ideological beliefs and/or their particular material interests. This results in a distorted discourse in which ideal speech conditions (see below) are undermined and rational argument avoided (or at least distorted).

When their own opinions or interests are being questioned, the powerful, the influential and the articulate will often have the means to manipulate, dominate or even determine an argument - and thereby override any rational points of view being put forward by others. In most instances, there is an asymmetrical set of power relations within competitive decision groups that favours some arguments at the expense of others. In such a 'distorted' discourse, deep-seated areas of potential agreement about legitimate interests, moral values and ethical practices can get ignored

[99] http://www.goodreads.com/quotes/328238

in the rough and tumble of surface level arguments about narrow, short-term priorities. Ironically, in recent times, this emphasis on immediacy and materiality is sometimes reinforced by well-meaning attempts to be inclusive. By holding a one-off referendum or carrying out consultation exercises with service users or other stakeholders concerned to further their own current interests, we may simply be reinforcing the justification for taking a narrow, short-term view of what to do.

In institutional settings, institutional norms and established role relationships determine, to a considerable extent, what gets done and how things happen. Day-to-day social interactions are also governed by these behavioural codes and conventions[100] (albeit in a less formal fashion). In normal everyday discourse, these formal and informal codes remain largely unquestioned: they are just accepted as being the way things are. Forms of legitimation that stem from these established norms and customs is a central feature of competitive discourse. In generative discourse, a different form of legitimation emerges. Because generative discourse is concerned to shift the emphasis from compromised agreement to inter-subjective understanding, it necessarily requires actors to consider all the legitimate concerns of all the stakeholders associated with the decision under consideration. In short, the generative discourse shifts the focus of attention away from questions of legitimate influence and towards questions of legitimate interests.

'Legitimate' influence

In a normal competitive discourse, even when asymmetrical power relations are felt to be unfair or unhelpful, their inevitability is more or less taken as given and this passive recognition gives them a sort of de facto legitimacy. The fact that some people or groups are better positioned than others to utilise established institutional conventions and arrangements to advocate their points of view is not openly discussed – it is just accepted as the way things are. Of course, in many instances there will be good reasons for some people to be allowed more influence than others – but in a truly open discourse, these reasons would be identified and legiti-

[100] Famously explored by Erving Goffman (1959) in The Presentation of Self in Everyday Life. Anchor Books.

mated through discussion early on in the decision-making process. More often than not, people are instinctively aware of how conventional social relationships work in real world situations: they know when their ideas and suggestions are not being listened to or when someone is 'using the system' to push through a proposal that has not been 'properly' debated. Established procedures, administrative arrangements and routines are understood by all concerned - and thereby form part of people's embedded assumptions about how things get done. Arguably the most obvious example of this sort of institutional power is derived from a person's rank, title or formal authority. There is an old story (probably apocryphal), that many years ago, at an ancient Oxbridge college, a meeting of the Fellows was convened by the Master to decide whether or not to change the constitution so as to allow women to be admitted for the first time to study for degrees. The vote was taken by a show of hands and all the Fellows voted in favour of the motion except the elderly Master himself who voted against. Having looked around the room, the Master declared, "Well gentlemen, we seem to be deadlocked". In this case, agency (in the form of a vote) operated within existing institutional arrangements (the college constitution that gave the Master the power to veto) to keep things as they are. On that day, the student admission arrangements remained unaltered.[101] The decision to admit women was postponed to a later date when a new younger and more liberally minded Master was in place. When this occurred, the forces of structuration (human agents operating within established institutional structures) again reproduced the undergraduate admission arrangements – but this time, they were not only reproduced - they were also transformed. Sudden transformative change is a rare event – but every hour of every day institutions and their arrangements are reproduced in slightly altered ways by what people say and do. Over time, small changes transform the social, economic, political and legal structures within which we live and work. Put simply, by dissolving agency into structure ("structuration"), discourse both reproduces and changes the social world and over time these incremental changes transform institutions and cultural conventions.

The freedom of some to use asymmetrical influence is dependent upon other people accepting their legitimacy to do so. Surface

[101] In the language of critical social theory – 'were reproduced in their current form'.

This notion of structurated reproduction was developed by Giddens A. (1982) Profiles and Critiques in Social Theory, Macmillan, pp.9/10. Berger and Luckmann developed a similar notion. They point out that even at the level of the solitary individual acting outside of any institutional setting, "habitualised actions" can provide a background of routinized activity that "opens up a foreground for deliberation and innovation". Through discourse the actor can contribute to maintaining the status quo – "let's carry on doing it as we've always done it." Or they can help to change the ways things are – "Let's do it a bit differently because..... "[Berger P. and Luckmann T. (1979). The Social Construction of Reality, Peregrin edition.] In other words, how agents engage with established social structures will determine the extent to which those social arrangements stay the same or change.

arguments about intentions and short-term priorities take place in social and institutional settings in which assumptions already exist about how decisions are normally made and arguments normally resolved. Although some of this asymmetrical power is overt and blunt - "I am your line manager and you will do as I say" – much of it is opaque and elusive. There is an important distinction to be made between ranked, uncompromising authority and subtle, discursive influence. Whenever someone engages with a more senior colleague or social superior, despite his or her apparent weaker position of influence, that lower ranked individual will normally be able to exercise some influence over how the meeting pans out. By being knowledgeable about 'what is going on' and 'how things are habitually done', all concerned are able to exercise some degree of control over the outcomes of the encounter. This subtle influence rests on social structural features that are essentially discursive in nature – and this is an important point. It is important because it means that these features are not so much static concrete constraints built into a hierarchy of power, but rather dynamic recurring patterns of interaction that flow through any stratified hierarchy. In this way, all participants in the encounter, no matter where they are ranked in the official hierarchy, have access to at least some 'discursive resources'. It is this linguistic fluidity that begins to open up the possibility of a different and more open way of interacting that rests on a different and more open way of thinking about legitimation.

LEGITIMATE INTERESTS

When interaction becomes so open that everyone is aware of the discursive dynamics, then the inequalities of rank and status inevitably become moderated and in some instances the current legitimacy is undermined altogether.

The notion of 'legitimation' has a different (and arguably more authentic) meaning when used in the context of generative discourse than it does in the context of competitive discourse. In multiple rationality analysis, a 'legitimate interest' is one that is appreciated and accepted by other actors and stakeholders even if such an acceptance contradicts the logical principles of their own specialized forms of knowledge (e.g. technical or professional logic) [102] or works against their own opinions or distinctive interests.[103] The underlying logic behind this position runs as follows.

When a social policy is based on reasoning that fails to take appropriate account of the legitimate interests of all those who will be affected, that reasoning constitutes a distorted discourse and the outcome of that reasoning results in a dysfunctional policy. This is because by failing to take account of these legitimate interests, such policies are not fully accepted and therefore they cannot be regarded as 'sustainable'.

A dysfunctional policy that comes from a distorted discourse is not sustainable because its failure to take proper account of legitimate interests is likely to result in the enacted outcome being challenged

an ironic paradox

some time in the future. This is not to say that everyone's interests have to be accommodated by a sustainable policy. It is to say, however, that if the strategic thinking and planning that preceded the enactment unreasonably ignored (or underplayed) some legitimate interests and opinions, this will come back to haunt those charged with implementing and carrying out the policy. It creates what might be thought of as an ironic paradox whereby the compet-

[102] Discussed in Garnett (1995). An example might be when a director of finance says, "This decision makes no sense financially, but I can see that legally we have to go with it".....or the director of technology says, "We could make the machine operate more effectively, but I can see that this is the best we can afford".

[103] An example might be when someone says "I don't like this decision, but I can see that your need is greater than mine, so I'll go along with it".

itive 'winner', by failing to incorporate what are felt to be legitimate concerns, eventually creates a reason for challenging the policy. This is a common issue where a social policy impacts on future generations or the interests of other absent voices.[104]

Structure and Agency: Dualism or Duality?

It is a particularly naïve teacher who believes that the children under his or her charge exercise no influence over the way a planned lesson unfolds. Destitute refugees have some capacity, however small, to influence how life is organised inside their hostels and holding camps and even prisoners have some capacity to engage in institutional life in ways that influence how their prisons are run. At the other end of overt power relations, every elected politician knows that to be successful, even presidents and prime ministers have to be constantly aware of the capacity to influence events that resides with their cabinet colleagues, senates, and constituencies. In this way we can regard all parties to an interaction as having a capacity to utilise their knowledge of the situation to influence social and institutional life through what critical social theorists term "the duality of structure".

In the social theory literature the idea of 'structure and agency' operating in harness to reproduce social arrangements has become an influential notion. In multiple rationality analysis this apparent dualism is conceived of as a discursive process. In this way it becomes possible to see the tensions between 'structural' and 'voluntaristic' forces pointed to by many writers, being dissolved in practice. In other words, the dualism that mainstream theory assumes to exist

In the social theory literature, there can be some confusion about the use of the terms 'dualism' and 'duality' and they are sometimes treated as a distinction without a difference. However, in rationality analysis they are not used interchangeably. When something is composed of two distinctive elements, we point to there being a 'dualism'. When we identify two different aspects of the same thing, we point to a 'duality'.

[104] See Garnett (1995), Multiple Rationality Analysis: An Approach to Reconciling the Competing Values and Interests Associated with Housing Renewal Schemes, Commonwealth Association of Surveying and Land Economy and The International Federation of Surveyors, 'Sustainable Development: Counting the Cost - Maximising the Value'. Harare, Zimbabwe, August 1995.

between people's actions on the one hand and the structural arrangements and habits within which these actions take place on the other, is dissolved into a duality. Structuration theory seeks to explain how the dualism of constraint and enablement (structure and agency)

Critics of Giddens's structuration theory argue that, in fact, social structure has a material reality that precedes, and is constitutive of, the taken-for-granted worlds into which we are born. They cite the crucial role of ideology and culture in normalising discrimination, legitimising social inequality and obscuring the barriers to legitimate opportunity for disadvantaged social groups in a patriarchal, racially discriminatory, class-divided society. Thus, social structure and human agency are not seen as just two sides of the same coin, as the dualists contend, because social structure has objective features which shape the destiny of individuals in profound ways. As a result, they say, the two realms of social structure and human agency must be analysed separately.

becomes resolved into a duality in real life social settings.

The conditions of an ideal speech situation

The discursive power of influence of which we speak is stronger the more it operates under conditions that approximate to those of an ideal speech situation. This is a crucial point and needs some further discussion.

Generative discourse seeks to establish a degree of inter-subjective understanding by tapping into a deeper cognitive level than the surface level argument. Where a competitive argument becomes irreconcilable, the continual restating of intransigent points of view is more likely to reinforce polarised positions than move things on. The most obvious general example of this is where people agree on what outcome is being sought (e.g. fairness, sustainability, intergenerational justice, best value, etc.) but disagree about the method of achievement. Because the continuous restating of surface arguments may deepen antagonisms and lead to noisier, more aggressive and more distorted forms of discourse, an agreement to begin the strategic thinking 'somewhere else' – at a deeper cognitive level – might open up opportunities for progress towards a resolution. This, however, presupposes certain discursive requirements.

The academic literature on the subject often models these

requirements by reference to Jurgen Habermas's notion of 'the ideal speech situation'. The ideal speech situation exists when those who are party to an argument willingly follow "rules of discourse" which collectively describe an intuition about what it means to be in a form of communicative interaction in which conflict would be resolved solely by the force of better argument. Generative discourse is grounded in deliberative codes of practice that consciously and systematically seek to facilitate free and open discussion that allows the full range of meanings of contested concepts to be expressed and understood.

We are arguing that it is through the duality of structure and agency that institutional practices are said to 'happen' or be 'made to happen' - not only in decision meetings, but also in the continuity of everyday life.[105] A simple way of looking at this is to say that in social settings people have unequal influence and authority that is not necessarily associated with their social standing, title, grade, or job description. To emphasise this point, we have asserted (above) that even in such environments as prisons, the inmates have a degree of power to change existing institutional cultures and practices. This is a subtle and somewhat counterintuitive claim because much of this situated power is embedded in established cultural conventions ("this is how we do things around here"). Socio-psychological predispositions and attitudes of acceptance both stem from, and are legitimated by, this culture.

The obvious danger of operating within a discourse that is distorted by prevailing procedures and conventions is that its lack of rational debate might produce an avoidably bad outcome. A distorted discourse resolves arguments and makes decisions and because it can achieve this in ways that are accepted as being legitimate, these decisions are normally not challenged at the time. As George Bernard Shaw may have put it, "The single biggest problem in communication is the illusion that it has taken place".[106] Our point is that a bad idea sanctioned by convention remains a bad idea. However, when a bad idea is recognised for what it is,

[105] Considered in this way, it becomes possible to treat power as a modality of structuration: that is, as a feature of both institutional arrangements and human agency as constituted in and through recurrent practices.

[106] Usually attributed to GBS, but more likely first published by William H. Whyte in Fortune. 'Is Anybody Listening?' P.174 New York: Time Inc. (September 1950).

people tend to react. Agents are intimately involved in the continuous reproduction of institutional practices and it is this involvement that enables current structural features to alter so that over time we move from the observation that "this is how we do things here" to "this is how we used to do things here but it's different and better now". As people engage with the structural properties (rules, roles, habitual practices, etc.) of an organisation those properties are both reproduced and altered. In this way, we can say that structuration is the engine of change that continuously reshapes social and institutional settings.

To make an analogy with Adam Smith's famous allusion, we might say that institutional practices and arrangements operate as a sort of "hidden hand" within a competitive discourse that unassumingly operates to resolve institutional arguments. Indeed, a competitive discourse displays many of the organizational features of a competitive market. The hidden forces of established traditions and ways of doing things resolve discursive disagreements by the competitive interplaying of arguments and counterarguments within a network of power relations. In terms of process, this is analogous to the way in which the market mechanism resolves any bickering over prices by the interplay of supply and demand. An important point we might take from this analogy is that just as the market can only be relied upon to provide an equilibrium price (that is assumed to be 'fair') so long as it is operating under the conditions of perfect competition, the competitive discourse can only be relied upon to provide an inter-subjective consensus (that is assumed to be 'sustainable') so long as it is operating under ideal speech conditions.

Generative Discourse: From Entrenched Opinion to Considered Best Practice

In his book Diplomacy (ominously published in 1939), Harold Nicolson took a long-term historical view of what constitutes "good' and 'bad' diplomacy thereby hoping "to indicate to the reader that the art of negotiation requires a combination of certain special qualities which are not always to be found in the ordinary politician,

a realistic way forward given all the circumstances

nor even in the ordinary man". He observed that throughout the ages opinions differed on the question as to whether intelligence or character, cunning or probity are more effective instruments of diplomacy. He challenged the cynical definition of a diplomat as 'someone paid to lie on behalf of his or her country' and argued that, in the long run, effective diplomacy rests on trust and honesty.

If competitive discourse can be said to be about negotiated compromise then generative discourse is about trust and mutual understanding. The distinction between competitive and generative discourse is always a matter of degree. Interactions are seldom purely competitive and participants in conventional decision meetings do sometimes show a degree of openness: as part of their negotiation it is not unknown for parties to a competitive discourse to make some reference to their underlying values and interests either directly as positive belief statements or indirectly as anxiety statements (scepticism). Such openness, however, is likely to be partial, arbitrary and random. By contrast, in generative discourse actors make an explicit commitment to open and creative thinking,[107] making their value predispositions transparent and actively seeking to reduce any communicative distortions that may arise from the social or institutional setting within which the discourse is taking place. We might say that in generative discourse, to some degree at least, structuration's 'hidden hand' is exposed and as a result, is less able to inhibit creative thinking.

Sustainable decisions emerge from discourses that are structured to produce warranted assertions that are arrived at through the force of better argument rather than through competitive negotiation. What is being sought is a form of discursive interaction that puts an emphasis on creativity and seeks sustainable proposals rather than settling for compromises between existing (competing) ideas. In other words, what is sought is the yet-to-be-thought 'sustainable' option: that is, a proposal that all parties accept as a realistic way forward and – given all the circumstances – is the 'best' that can be done. This may take the form of a considered second best compromise of one of the envisioned 'ideals' already on the table. On the other hand, it may take the form of a newly generated option that had not been considered up to that point. The over-arching question being: 'Is there a realistic way forward that we have not yet considered and that is more appropriate

[107] The term 'open' here indicates that the discourse aspires to create the conditions of Habermas's ideal speech situation. It also indicates a situation in which all assertions can be subjected to unrestricted scrutiny.

than any of the options that have so far been proposed?' Clearly, such a question cannot be addressed through the mechanism of a competitive discourse where individuals put all their energies into defending predetermined views and constantly repeating previously presented proposals.

Although a competitive discourse may lead to a compromised existing view being accepted, it is unlikely to produce an altogether new way forward. By utilising embedded asymmetrical power relations, it can decide between existing options, but a competitive discourse is unlikely to generate new ones. A generative discourse is not concerned with compromises that lead to the adoption of a policy that all regard as 'second best' - but with establishing inter-subjective understandings that lead to the taking of decisions and the creation of policies that, after full and open deliberation, all accept IS the best.

Talking to the Elephant

Generative discourse involves the application of multiple rationality analysis. The first step in applying multiple rationality analysis is for all concerned to recognise that the surface arguments of a competitive discourse are, to some considerable extent, derived from underlying personal or group attitudes and values. In decision-making, these deeper-seated attitudes are seldom brought into view but shelter in the safe silence of conventional taciturnity where they remain protected from scrutiny. They are, we might say, the 'elephants in the room' that everyone knows are there but are ignored.

An 'elephant in the room' represents a serious issue that is being ignored or avoided because it would be inconvenient or politically or socially embarrassing to discuss it openly. The phrase is often used to refer to an issue involving a social taboo such as assumed racial or gender stereotyping or religious beliefs. It is sometimes said to exist because people are overly concerned not to offend other people's sensitivities or to be charged with being 'politically incorrect'. More often it is other people's legitimate concerns that are avoided for fear of weakening one's own argument. The rogue elephant that is of most concern to us in this discussion is the reluctance to confront an opinion that is overtly illogical or demonstrably false.

Where there are ingrained differences of opinion, these will be apparent to everyone. This means that all concerned can at least agree on something - namely that policy differences exist. Of course, in deadlocked discussions this self-evident fact is well understood but where the mode of the discussion is competitive, this recognition takes us nowhere: it is no more than a statement of the obvious. For those advocating a shift away from a competitive towards a generative mode of discussion, however, this situation offers a Donald Rumsfeld type of optimistic paradox: the more fervent the disagreement, the stronger the agreement that disagreement exists. In competitive situations, this obvious realisation might provide a polite but inconclusive way of ending the discourse – "Well let's leave it there - at least we can agree to disagree". At this point competitive forces come into play and a (later to be regretted) decision is imposed. The 'optimistic'

By engaging the elephant in the discussion, concepts are challenged and mind-sets can alter in ways that can produce a more robust and sustainable decision.

contention of multiple rationality analysis, however, is that under certain circumstances, the recognition of deadlock can constitute a starting point for a new way of engaging that will result in a sustainable decision – or at least a decision that brings in its wake fewer regrets. The required condition for this optimism is an acceptance by all to participate more generatively and less competitively. An important part of this shift involves introducing the elephant in the room to the decision group and then inviting it to take part in the discussion.

The hope is that through multi-rational thinking and analysis we can arrive at some form of inter-subjective understanding that can form the basis of a sustainable decision. The principles of multi-rational thinking require the deliberative process to be carried out in an atmosphere of openness. That is, all the participants should seek, as far as possible, to emulate the ideal speech situation with the conscious (indeed declared) intention of reconciling competing claims to right action. Our optimistic proposition that 'creative reconciliation is possible' is based on the assumption that many disputed claims are grounded in contested - but not essentially contested – concepts. In other words, 'X' may

Contested Concepts

In a paper delivered to the Aristotelian Society on 12 March 1956, Walter Bryce Gallie introduced the term "essentially contested concept" as a way of identifying those qualitative notions (such as 'beauty', 'truth' and 'social justice') that permeate the domains of aesthetics, religion and political philosophy, and over which there exists no fixed, agreed understanding of what they mean. In MRA we draw an important distinction between what we are terming 'contested concepts' and 'essentially contested concepts'.

A contested concept or idea is one that is used to mean different things by different people in different contexts. In many cases (e.g. 'sustainable', 'best', 'efficient', etc.), it is not so much a 'contested' meaning as an ambiguous and imprecise one. Its key characteristic is that, once the context of its use is understood, agreement about its meaning (in that context) can be achieved.

An essentially contested concept or notion is one that has a meaning that is fundamentally disputed (in any context). In some instances, it is "essentially contested" in the sense that the very structure of its meaning is disagreed on by social commentators (e.g. 'evolution', 'consciousness', etc.). In some instances there can exist a general understanding of the broad nature of a concept such as 'fairness', 'effectiveness', etc., but not on how best to realise an assumed beneficial outcome (e.g. a 'fair distribution of income' or an 'effective housing policy'). In other words, concepts can be "essentially contested" in terms of either definition or application (or both). The key feature of an essentially contested concept is that disputes about its meaning or appropriate application cannot be settled by an appeal to empirical evidence, linguistic usage, or the rules of logic. Essentially contested claims are irreconcilable. Essentially contested disputes stem from religious convictions or fundamental beliefs or attitudes rather than from contextual misunderstandings.

MRA's 'optimistic' proposition that in many instances "reconciliation is possible" is based on the assumption that contested claims are grounded in contested, but not essentially contested, concepts. The assumption being made in MRA is that, even though their interests and values may never coincide, people holding different views can, through open discourse, come to understand each other's meaning(s) of the concept(s) being used and that this understanding can provide the basis for generating an agreed course of action. This understanding can be thought of as being inter-subjective.

disagree with 'Y' that a particular asserted course of action is 'just' or 'socially efficient' or 'environmentally friendly', etc., because their different interests and values are such that in presenting their particular arguments, they are each relying on discretely different meanings of the notions of 'justice', 'efficiency, 'friendliness', etc. However, even though their interests and values may never coincide, because they share mutual[108] knowledge about how to communicate effectively, they can, through open discussion, come to appreciate each other's subjectively understood meaning of the contested concept(s) being employed. It is this appreciation that provides the basis for generating an agreed course of action that will not, at some future date, be regretted.

Generative discourse is grounded in deliberative codes of practice that consciously and systematically seek to facilitate free and open discussion that allows essentially contested concepts to be recognised and put to one side and the full range of meanings of contested concepts to be expressed and then inter-subjectively understood. By committing to multiple rationality analysis, all those taking part in the exercise automatically sign up to this intention to cultivate a working environment of openness and shared understandings. Establishing this commitment constitutes the first stage of an MRA exercise. The second is to generate yet-to-be-thought options that all agree might be in the best long-term interests of all concerned: this takes us into the field of strategic thinking. Strategic thinking is not the same thing as strategic planning.[109] It precedes the planning and implementation of policy. In the current management language, it is concerned with 'strategic mission, vision and values' rather than with 'operations and tactical goals'.

professional interests tied up with issues

The main problem with competitive discourse is that it produces winners and losers. Although a decision is reached, loser discontent persists and it is this persistence of dissatisfaction that makes the decision unstable and, in some instances, unsustainable. In order to make progress through a more generative approach there has

[108] See chapter 2.
[109] See Appendix 2.

to be recognition by all concerned that it is underlying attitudes rather than surface level proposals that are preventing the formation of a sustainable agreement. For a proposal to be genuinely sustainable, different rationalities must be reconciled through an inter-subjective agreement that, although the final decision is not what all (or possibly any) concerned were arguing for, it is nevertheless 'warranted' and, given the socio-political reality of the situation, the best outcome that can be achieved. Clearly this generative reconciliation requires some form of rationality analysis to take place. For rationality analysis to take place, there has to be an explicit commitment, first to appreciate that the surface discussions are deadlocked and then to understand that, despite this, reconciliation may yet be achievable if the competitive approach is abandoned for a form of discussion that addresses deeper cognitive concerns in a way that is open and creative. The word "generative" in the context being discussed here points to two closely interrelated features of open discourse. It indicates that such a discourse seeks to be creative and, more specifically (and pragmatically), it signifies a commitment to create new options rather than appraise existing options.

In a competitive discourse, professional knowledge as well as personal attitudes can impact on the discussion. It is often arguments about circumscribed instrumental interests that tend to constitute the primary subject matter of the interchanges. These are often derived from the various professional concerns within the decision group. The professional concerns (priorities) of the director of finance may differ from those of the I.T. or sales team for example. The discourse is more likely to concentrate on disagreements about methods of implementation than on fundamental objectives. "We both want to do the right thing – but your proposal won't work/ is unfair/ is inefficient/ can't be afforded/ etc....." Because so many conflicting personal ideologies and material and professional interests are tied up with issues of implementation (or the decision whether or not to implement), much argument concentrates on 'How or if we're going to do it' rather than with 'What we're really trying to achieve'. In this way, the competitive decision discourse provides a mechanism for arguing over preconceived options and strategic planning issues rather than providing an opportunity to do some strategic thinking and to generate better, yet-to-be-thought-of, options. Competitive discourse is about compromise while generative discourse pursues inter-subjective agreement.

Generative Discourse: Transformative Idea or Naïve Hope?

At first sight, the argument that it is possible to have an open debate under ideal speech conditions seems naïve because it is generally assumed that money, rank and established conventions will always favour the arguments of the powerful over those of the not so powerful. To put it more bluntly, it is said to be unreasonable to suggest that rational argument can override established power relations. To argue this, however, is to miss the point. We are not here arguing that it is possible to achieve the ideal speech situation but that such a situation is an ideal theoretical communicative state to which we should aspire if we want to achieve a deep agreement grounded in inter-subjective understandings.

Inter-subjectivity

This is a term used in philosophy, psychology, sociology, and anthropology to emphasise the fact that rational social actions are grounded in shared social meanings. It is used in contrast to solipsistic individual understandings and its use emphasises the inherently social nature of human experience. Rational analysts seek to make decisions that are based on inter-subjective understandings. In other words, it is argued that the competitive discourse is not so much a dynamic (creative) exercise as a static (entrenched) power fight. Each of the preconceived instrumental proposals will, of course, be linked in some way to a deeper-seated personal system of values and beliefs but – and this is the point – a competitive discourse fails to make these embedded attitudes available for 'full and proper' consideration. The failure to give a proposal's underlying moral rationalisations 'proper' consideration does not mean that people's beliefs and ideological leanings play no part in the discourse. Quite the reverse: the discourse will often be largely driven by entrenched attitudinal stances - but again the point is that they remain obscure, largely unexamined and unchallenged. In the field of governance and decision-making, agreement is not the same thing as consensus. True consensus is produced through an open discourse that requires everyone recognising the need to find a creative synthesis that is something more than a simple compromise. Ideally it represents an outcome of which most people approve, nobody hates and everybody respects. Both the meaning and mechanics of such a discourse hinge on the notion of 'openness'.

An analogy can be made with the economist's notion of a perfectly competitive market. Although such a market seldom if ever occurs in the real knock-about world of commerce, the conditions that would need to be present to achieve perfect competition have to be identified if we want to be able to assess the actual degree of competition that exists in a particular real-life market. Similarly, although all the conditions of the ideal speech situation can never exist, we need to identify what those conditions would be if we wish to approximate them in practice.

We are arguing that when the ability to make a sustainable decision is inhibited by differences of opinion, we should shift to a more creative approach to discourse that emulates the conditions of an ideal speech situation. It is under these conditions that decision-makers seek to reconcile their rationalising arguments in a process of strategic thinking that we are terming 'multiple rationality analysis' (MRA). The key proposition is that if the participants in a decision discourse are explicit about the values, attitudes and interests that lie behind their propositional statements, they will arrive at a 'deeper' understanding about what courses of action should be put forward for consideration and appraisal.[110] It is from this proposition that we derive the hypothesis that the 'deeper' (more critically aware) understanding will lead to more robust decisions. Arguably, the single most problematic aspect of this approach centres on the ability people have to understand the sources of their own and other people's values, attitudes and opinions. To put it bluntly, we cannot be explicit about that of which we are not aware. Although this is a real problem (arguably the greatest weakness in our argument), it should not be used as a reason to avoid attempts to analyse how and why arguments are being rationalized. After all, a degree of self-awareness is a necessary element of any philosophical position.

[110] A 'deep consensus' is being defined as an agreement arrived at through open deliberation that incorporates an appreciation of other people's legitimate values and interests. The practical benefits of this approach were pointed to by Michel Barnier, the EU's chief Brexit negotiator, when, at the end of the first negotiating session, he complained that the British position lacked clarity. He went on to say that, "quite simply, we are making most progress in those areas where our respective positions have been made clear." (20 July 2017)

Self Awareness

In the first century A.D. the ex-slave and teacher Epictetus maintained that the foundation of all philosophy is self-knowledge and that without it, no other form of knowledge is possible. "First learn the meaning of what you say, and then speak." (Epictetus).

This ancient insight forms the basis of our argument here. The bringing together of individual viewpoints and attitudes to create some form of inter-subjective understanding is clearly not possible without a prior appreciation of our own and other people's subjective beliefs and forms of reasoning. [This issue is explored further in the next chapter.]

From theory to practice

Critical theory points to the following necessary conditions to establish an *ideal speech situation.*

*Each participant must be equally positioned within the social structure of the dialogue: in particular, no-one must be allowed to dominate or have a specially advantageous role at the discussion table.

*For all participants there must be an equality of opportunity to select and employ speech acts.[111] In particular, they must have equal opportunity to express their attitudes, feelings, hopes and fears, etc., ask questions, challenge and support other people's propositional statements, and proffer explanations and justifications of their own statements without feeling inhibited or threatened.

In other words,

> "..... the conditions of the ideal speech situation must insure not only unlimited discussion but also discussion which is free from all constraints of domination, whether their source be conscious strategic behaviour or communication barriers secured in ideology and neurosis." McCarthy 1976 p.xvii Translator's introduction to Legitimation Crisis: Jürgen Habermas.

Although an effective MRA exercise needs to take place within a coordinating framework, in common with brainstorming techniques such as SWOT or GAP analysis, it is essentially an

[111] The notion of speech acts is taken from John R.Searle (1969 – reprinted 2012: CUP) who used the term to refer to the basic unit of linguistic analysis. Examples of speech acts would include making statements, asking questions, proffering answers, giving commands and making promises.

open-minded activity. It is a discursive arrangement in which the participants seek to create an inter-subjective understanding of the nature and scope of key value objectives in the context of the project under review. From this, it is expected that 'yet-to-be-thought-of' options will be generated. Although an MRA discussion should be fluid and open (rather than procedural and structured), its operation does involve the application of four fundamental principles:

1. The discussion should focus on an over-arching contested concept or set of concepts (such intergenerational justice, sovereignty, sustainability, etc.).
2. The participants should seek to establish a shared understanding of the contested concept's meaning in the context of the decision under review.
3. A disinterested party should facilitate this initial discussion.
4. The participants should move towards agreement by means of a staged discursive process that distinguishes between 'option generation' and 'option appraisal'.

Of course, the key question now arises: 'How, in practical terms, do we go about analysing multiple rationalities?' By committing to MRA all those taking part in the exercise automatically sign up to this intention to cultivate a working culture of openness. Establishing this shared commitment constitutes the first stage of an MRA exercise.

It has to be understood that MRA has its roots in the traditions of critical theory rather than objectivism. That is, its basic tenets come from that school of thought that rejects the possibility of a value-free social science and, instead, adopts a theoretical perspective that assumes the possibility of the communication processes leading to a "deep" understanding of values. This means that it should not be regarded as a technique for appraising policy proposals against some pre-understood measure of efficacy, objectivity or truth - but rather as an approach to achieving policy agreement in a way that embraces the social and politico-theoretical dimension of real-world decision-making. Just as empiricist and objectivist methodologies seek to set judgement above human interests and values, MRA accepts the fundamental irrationality of this endeavour and seeks to reconcile particular interests and values through a systematic, but 'open', deliberative procedure that, at an early stage, requires each party to the discourse to explicate what they understand by such notions as 'sustainability', 'accountability', 'inclusiveness', etc., in the context of the project being considered.

The question arises - 'How to set up the conditions that will

There is no one definitive way of analysing multiple rationalities. Indeed, we might argue that MRA is more a mind-set than a technique. This text is concerned to lay out the case for a generative approach to policy formation rather than provide a manual for how to go about its achievement. However, any reader wishing to explore some of the practical issues associated with carrying out an MRA exercise should check out the following reference: Garnett D (2020), Multiple Rationality Analysis: An Introduction, leapingfrogpublications.co.uk

accommodate generative discourse?' The precise arrangements will necessarily be tailored to the nature and scope of the issues being addressed. However, given MRA's commitment to critical analysis, it is appropriate and possible to identify a number of key operational principles that will apply to any MRA exercise.

In attempting to identify the underlying, requisite codes of practice of MRA, we turn to the conditions that critical theorists say need to be established to produce the ideal speech situation. In this, we are seeking to ensure that the "pragmatic structure of communication" (Habermas) is such that the deliberations are free from those "accidental or systematic constraints on discussion" (McCarthy in Habermas 1976) that stand in the way of the emergence of a shared rationality that can become the basis of a 'deep' agreement about what to propose as constituting right action (warranted assertion). The optimistic hope is that MRA can provide a mechanism for transforming democratic ideals into practice so that which is desirable can be imagined and once imagined, acted upon. By such a commitment to the imagination the life-chances of current and future citizens may be enhanced by social polices that we do not live to regret.

Chapter 7

Making Assertions

"Watch your own speech, and notice how it is guided by your less conscious purposes."
(George Eliot)

For you and me to participate in an undistorted discourse I need to understand not only what you think, but also why you think what you think and you need to understand why I think what I think. From this inter-subjective understanding and exposure of our beliefs and values, we can work more effectively together towards some sort of agreement about what should be done for the best. If a concord is arrived at by such an open mechanism, we might regard the conclusion as "deep" and "sustainable". By contrast, we should regard a policy decision arrived at by a competitive process of partially reasoned assertions as "surface" and "temporary". In practical policy-making, people often behave as protagonists and as such they debate in generalisations and make assertions - but to produce sustainable outcomes, generalisations have to be worked for. Assertions have to be justified and the justifications have to be understood rather than simply asserted. In the last chapter we made the point that arguably the greatest barrier to achieving ideal speech conditions is an inability to understand the nature and scope of the prejudices and preconceptions that underlie our own and other people's assertions. In this and the next chapter we will consider this problem more fully.

Some barriers to open communication are more problematic than others. Gore Vidal told a story about a diplomatic incident when, together with their wives, Harold Macmillan and Charles De Gaulle were having dinner. They were discussing what they were looking forward to doing once they had left office. The British Prime Minister noticed that De Gaulle's wife Yvonne was not saying anything and, to bring her into the conversation, he asked her directly what she was looking forward to. She replied, somewhat bluntly "a penis". Taken aback, Macmillan suffered a few moments of embarrassed silence before urbanely moving the discussion on. De Gaulle then leaned over and said, "What Madame means is "'Appiness".

We are not concerned with those open and obvious barriers to communication that stem from mispronunciations or other surface-level linguistic misunderstandings. Our concern is to expose, and subsequently find ways of reducing, those frictions that occur in discursive interactions that inhibit the achievement of an ideal speech situation.. In many respects, it is the speaker or listener rather than the structure of the speech that gets in the way of fully open discourse. In his Autobiography, John Stuart Mill makes reference to what he termed "intuitionism" which he saw as people's inclination to believe that their ethical judgements are based on some innate, a priori set of underlying values. Mill regarded this tendency as dangerous because it enables people to ratify their particular prejudices as moral principles without any reference to an external standard by which to judge competing claims to truth (or 'right action'). Modern commentators refer to the tendency to seek out examples that support an existing preconception as confirmation bias.

When we engage in dialogue, discussion or debate we bring to the table not only our arguments, but also ourselves: indeed, who we are plays a large part in determining what we say. This is a well-established observation. As the philosopher G. E. Moore argued at the beginning of the twentieth century, nothing whatsoever can take the place of reasoned justifications for the truth of a statement. Intuition, he argued, can only furnish a personal reason for holding a proposition to be true; it cannot provide a universally acceptable reason for claiming the truth of a proposition. Or to put it at its simplest: 'Good' means 'good' and that's all there is to say about it. Moore objected to something called 'the naturalistic fallacy', which states that moral truths can be analysed in terms of physical or psychological things that exist in the natural world. Moral truths were moral truths, and that was that.

> *"The evidence of a proposition to us is only a reason for our holding it to be true: whereas a logical reason, or reason in the sense in which self-evident propositions have no reason, is a reason why the proposition itself must be true, not why we hold it so to be.......We must not therefore look on Intuition as if it were an alternative to reasoning." (G.E.Moore 1903).*[112]

[112] G.E.Moore (1903), Principia Ethica: Cambridge: CUP. [2017 Reprint Amazon, p.122.]

Of course, Moore's point does not dismiss the significance of intuitionism.[113] Indeed, his statement might be said to reinforce the idea that there are real moral 'truths' that are not susceptible to analysis. It may well be the case that there are fundamental truths that cannot be broken down into parts or defined by reference to anything except other moral truths and we can only discover these by using our minds in a particular, intuitive way.

Our take on the world is largely derived from the habitus of our being (what we've become through personal experience) and this, as Schopenhauer pointed out, can mean that for everyone there is a tendency to take the limits of his or her own fields of vision for the limits of the world. Even when the objective facts are not in dispute, their social or political meanings are deduced through the filter of our individual predispositions and established opinions. Some of our perceptions have been acquired from our family and childhood friends and some of our more mature opinions will be acquired as we engage with moral arguments and ethical concerns later in life. At any one moment we see and judge the social world through an acquired interpretive prism. Critical theorists analyse these distorting prisms by reference to two interrelated general theories – the theory of habitus and standpoint theory.

Habitus and the general standpoint theory

Habitus For any individual, his or her age, class, ethnicity, gender, religion, up-bringing, education, employment, and place of residence are likely to interact in ways that create a distinctive attitude or "habitus". The idea of habitus is taken from Pierre Bourdieu who defined the notion as a "system of dispositions".[114] In French the semantic cluster of features that constitute "disposition" is rather wider than is implied by the English word. In employing the notion of habitus Bourdieu means to signify that which results from inculcating established values in a way that predisposes the individual to embrace certain attitudes and opinions. It can be thought of as a socially constituted system of cognitive and motivating structures that is implicated in the expressions of the deep-seated moral logic upon which an individual's

[113] See chapter 9.

[114] The notion is amplified in his influential book Outline of a Theory of Practice (Cambridge Studies in Social Anthropology, CUP 1972).

subjective judgements are built. Habitus plays a fundamental role in determining what a person understands to be right or wrong, ethical or unethical, reasonable or unreasonable, and so on.

Standpoint theory is a postmodern idea that makes the point that a person's position within a society has a particularly powerful effect on the shaping of his or her habitus. The theory emerged from the Marxist argument that people from an oppressed class have special access to knowledge (consciousness) that is not available to those from a privileged class. The contemporary contention is that in societies stratified by class and other categories such as race and gender, knowledge is always socially situated and our social position shapes what we can know. A critical theorist's take on standpoint theory might argue that knowledge may indeed partly stem from social situation but we have to be aware of the significance of belonging to cultural groupings that espouse clearly articulated ethical, religious or political points of view. The argument here is that people's judgements about what is right and just are partly determined, and constantly reinforced, by contact with others who see the world from a similar standpoint. Because the specifics of each person's position in society is unique, standpoint factors can only be regarded as having a generalised influence. Not all feminists, for example, are women and not all women are feminists. Similarly, in time of war, not all Christians are conscientious objectors and not all conscientious objectors are Christians. Having said this, standpoint theory suggests that both feminists and Christians perceive the world of social affairs through some sort of judgemental lens.

The commitment and the perception paradox

What we are here calling 'commitment theory' can be thought of as a sub-set of general standpoint theory that applies to people who have a predisposition to "change society for the better". The theory is not so much concerned with sentimental, reactive charitable instincts but more with people's positive desire to use political campaigning to make structural changes in society in line with their acquired views about what is decent and socially just. Over the years, activists have championed the rights of exploited and marginalised groups that they feel have been unfairly discriminated against on the basis of race, class or gender.

In order to give their campaigns a clear identity and more political purchase, some of these have created active research and lobbying groups. In the pursuit of intellectual legitimacy, these groups typically claim that their social analysis is neutral and objective and that they possess not only an understanding of the nature of discrimination, subordination and exploitation, but also of the factors that perpetuate them. These associations of concern and understanding can provide activists with both the psychological reassurance that accompanies a group identity and specific facilities that they can use to propagate their arguments for change.[115]

Some of these associations have taken the form of loosely organized large-scale campaigning movements (such as the nineteenth century anti-slavery and universal suffrage campaigns and the contemporary 'green' movement). Others have taken the form of more specifically organized pressure groups with highly focused agendas (such as Anti-Slavery International, the suffragettes and Friends of the Earth). These are all 'categories of commitment' that exist over and above any strict religious or party political, groups (such as the Catholic Church or the Republican Party, etc.). Their commitment tends to be intellectually combative rather than doctrinaire and typically they take the form of a semi-permanent campaign for change rather than a permanent association of believers.

The emergence of these social/cultural movements has created a contemporary paradox. Their current influence within disciplines such as history, sociology, ethics and cultural studies is now significant. A paradox exists in the sense that judging a social situation from a perspective that is intended to correct historically entrenched prejudice, can itself establish presuppositions that create judgemental distortions. As Estela Serret notes in her commentary on gender perspectives in education, "Above all, employing a gender perspective in politics implies a feminist view as a starting point."[116] The question arises: 'Does taking a committed perspective result in seeing social affairs through a correcting lens or through a distorting lens?' To put it crudely, does being a black activist, a

[115] Such as campaigns, websites, news letters, etc.

[116] Serret, Estela (2008). "¿Qué es la perspectiva de género?" in Qué es y para qué sirve la perspectiva de género. Textbook for the Perspectiva de género en la educación superior class at the Instituto de la Mujer Oaxaqueña, Oaxaca.

Marxist, an environmentalist or a feminist, predispose someone to make more rational or less rational judgements about social affairs?

We might argue that a problem of objectivity arises when an argument is derived from a 'committed' position. This was a famous concern of Howard Bloom who was concerned to reclaim literature from those critics he referred to as the "School of Resentment" who espoused a social purpose in reading.

> *"The idea that you benefit the insulted and injured by reading someone of their own origins rather than reading Shakespeare is one of the oddest illusions ever promoted by or in our schools.".*
> *(Howard Bloom 1994, The Western Canon).*

Bloom's position was that politics had no place in literary criticism, and that a feminist or Marxist reading of Hamlet would tell us something about feminism and Marxism but probably nothing about Hamlet itself.

When a self-declared feminist, Marxist (or any other "-ist") comments on some specific social issue, we might reasonably suspect that the speaker's global preconceptions and commitments are driving his or her judgment on the local issue in question. Those who question the legitimacy of standpoint theory claim that assumed knowledge is inevitably contextual and socially situated and this needs to be recognised in discussion. The suspicion is that a generalised commitment to a wider ethical or political campaign may be taking precedence over any focused analysis of the embedded complexities of the question being discussed. The concern might be that the (arguably worthy) generalisation acts as a distorting lens that skews the policy debate under review by ignoring its context or by preventing its associated policy dilemmas from being discussed objectively. The concern is that objective thinking can be impeded (or even blocked) by socially coerced attitudes being imposed by influential decision makers. To a greater or lesser extent, such people are bound to take note of a whole range of culturally embedded political sensitivities that feature in the current mega-discourse surrounding the local issue being discussed.

A media outcry followed the Metropolitan Police's 2012 Operation Yewtree Inquiry into historic allegations of extensive and persistent sexual abuse of 589 children and vulnerable adults by the TV personality Sir Jimmy Savile and others. The reaction of the Metropolitan Police to the furore was immediate and dramatic. Their subsequent approach to investigating such allegations changed so that they became much more predisposed to believe the accusations of possible victims and less inclined to believe automatically the denials of those accused – even when they were rich and eminent. This new attitude was soon to have unfortunate consequences.

Barely two years after Operation Yewtree, this new inclination (we might say 'commitment') of the police and other authorities to take on face value the claims of alleged child abuse produced a series of miscarriages of justice that destroyed the reputations of a number of eminent people who were wrongly accused of belonging to a VIP paedophile ring. A report into Scotland Yard's disastrous investigation revealed by the lawyer who led the independent inquiry into child sexual abuse warned detectives that the star witness was a probable liar, but he was ignored. The warning came in September 2015, six months before police wound up their inquiry and declared former military chief Lord Bramall, former home secretary Leon Brittan and former Conservative MP Harvey Proctor as innocent. We might say that the Savile experience[117] created a commitment reflex that prevented the police from perceiving that their key witness was a fantasist.

Understanding the options

More than most authorities in a free society, the police are liable to be sensitive to how they justify their actions. Indeed, in any accountable organisation, all decisions have to be justified and the justifications given are typically embedded in rationalisations that are in some way warranted:

'We should do this because: - it will increase our profits / boost staff morale / reduce our exposure to risk / be the fair and proper thing to do.....'.

[117] Reinforced by revelations of other paedophile activities of famous entertainers such as Garry Glitter and Rolf Harris.

Recently in Rotherham, Oxford, Rochdale (and elsewhere in England), the police were criticised for paying scant attention to the 'grooming' and sexual abuse of white girls and young women by men of Pakistani, Asian or Muslim origin. It was suggested that this was the result of concerns about appearing to be "racist". By the time that the offences took place, this concern about stereotyping was well established in the academic literature used in police training and in the qualifying courses for social workers and related welfare professionals. When some parliamentarians and the media expressed concerns that local politicians and the police were ignoring the serious nature and true impact of this form of offending, some academics were accused of defending the authorities by assuming that the reaction was an example of "moral panic". Best (2013) for example, suggested that the 'moral panic' argument may have been used by "political progressives" as a term of political abuse; that is - as an invidious label given largely on the basis of unstated ideological assumptions in order to discredit those who claim to have identified a social problem for which they sought an easily identifiable group to blame. Howard Becker's 1967 essay on this topic Whose Side Are We On? argued that where groups are ranked according to power and influence, "it is taken as given" that the highest status group will define the way things are regarded. John Kitsuse (1962) had made a similar point when he argued that deviance is not a property inherent in certain types of behaviour but a title conferred upon such behaviour by those who witnessed it or were in some way responsible for dealing with it.

More recently, the criminologist and researcher into gang behaviour John Pitts is one of a number of current commentators who are voicing concerns about the danger of side-lining the victimisation of young vulnerable women in an implicit appeal to higher loyalties wherein (evidence of harm to victims notwithstanding) academics see their primary responsibility as aiding the struggle against the demonization of socially disadvantaged social or ethnic minorities. (Pitts J. (2019) Street Grooming, Ethnicity and the Social Scientists, Pearce J. (ed.) Theoretical perspectives on Child Sexual Exploitation: The Contribution of Theory to Prevention & Intervention, Palgrave Macmillan).

However, the important question is not 'Was this decision rational?' but rather, 'How did this particular rationalisation come to dominate the argument?' By asking this question we draw attention to the fact that strategic thinking and planning do not start with the appraisal of options but with the generation of options. When options are generated through the distorting lens of misguided commitment, things can go badly wrong. Determining the appropriate option involves time, effort – and above all – freedom from predetermined assumptions.

Legitimate concerns might be said to exist when a course of action is simply asserted without being underpinned by any coherent rationalisation. In the current political climate of populist rhetoric it does appear that the justifications for some assertions are incoherent or devoid of cogent logical reasoning and rely for their validation on the subjective feelings of individuals and groups who believe that their emotion is justification enough for their wishes to be acted upon. Rationalists, of course, argue that being angry does not in itself constitute a reason to be heard and taken seriously. Having said this, throughout history a case has been made for arguing that sentiment, intuition and emotion can sometimes play a legitimate part in social argument.[118] At all times there have been those who vehemently argue that logic has its limitations and that full understanding cannot be achieved through reason alone: "reason only knows what reason knows". The emotional approach to argument can carry weight but should always be challenged where it is overtly irrational, is tied to a predisposition, or clearly contradicts the evidence.

The tension between emotion and reason stems from the proposition that there are two integral virtues of 'truth telling': (a) sincerity and (b) accuracy. The concerns underlying much of what we have argued in this text comes from a widely held perception that in recent times the balance between these two virtues has been disturbed to such an extent that we are making decisions that we will live to regret. To some of us, we seem to have entered into a public discourse in which sincerity is out-trumping accuracy in a way that is worrying. To overstate the case to make the point, we seem to be hearing in some quarters the belief that "so long as I'm sincere, I don't need to check the facts." There is a danger that by equating sincerity with authenticity it is being regarded as a virtue that stands on its own so that it is seen as a sufficient legitimation of a claim to truth – "I sincerely believe this to be true – therefore it must be true".

[118] Notably philosophers in the Romantic tradition (such as Rousseau) who believed in humanity's innate 'natural' virtues.

Where accountability is a key feature of the decision making process, there will always be a requirement to specify rational and coherent justifications for a proposed course of action that has significant consequences. Such justifications might be regarded as being particularly important in certain areas of policy formation or change, viz:

1. Where proposed constitutional changes would disturb the established governance principles or arrangements of a nation state or a private or public corporation. Examples might include altering executive powers, reducing or increasing the authority of the judiciary within a state, altering the articles of memorandum of a company, joining or leaving an international customs union, amalgamating with another organisation, etc. The significance of such changes may be recognised by the setting of special decision arrangements to gain approval such as a general election, the enactment of a statute, an annual (or special) general meeting, or some sort of a referendum. Where the proposed change is of this sort of significance, it has been the usual practice (until recently) to require any vote in favour to be greater than fifty per cent.

2. Where a proposed policy centres on a major ethical issue over which there exists deep-seated moral concerns. Included in this category would be such topics as abortion, capital punishment, genetic manipulation, euthanasia, etc. When compared to other policy debates, policy proposals in this category tend to be discussed in ways that unambiguously expose actors' values and attitudes. Those actively engaged in supporting or opposing policy propositions in this category often do so by making open and explicit reference to a religious belief or a fundamental principle.[119]

3. Where a proposal will profoundly affect the interests of individuals or groups (including minorities and future generations) - such as a significant change in taxation, large-scale public borrowing, compulsory purchase of tangible assets, or a major restructuring of the welfare system.

4. Where the policy involves proposals to carry out irreversi-

[119] *See chapter 8 for discussion on the notion of 'a principle'.*

ble infrastructure projects that would employ large amounts of non-renewable resources or impose significant social or environmental costs now and in the future. Such justifications are typically presented in the form of option appraisal reports that include reasoned arguments, cost-benefit analyses, environmental impact analyses, statistical data, research findings, etc.

5. Where the policy would be difficult or expensive to reverse if it were to be regretted once enacted.

In whatever form a policy proposal is finally presented, the justified course of action will normally have incorporated deliberative activities (language events) in which competing ideas and approaches will have been presented and considered. Strategies for action do not fall ready-made out of the sky but have to be formulated in closed or open debate between people who have a direct interest in what happens or who claim to have an expert knowledge of or have specified responsibilities for, the decision under consideration. In the field of social policy-making it is seldom possible to offer conclusive proof that a particular proposal constitutes 'best action'. Whatever their experience, expertise, or responsibilities, people cannot normally 'prove', in any scientific sense, that their ideas are 'correct' - the best they can do is to put forward warranted proposals and discuss them openly.

In democratically accountable decision groups various proposals are advanced, argued for and justified by making reference to specialised knowledge and overt interests. The arguments and justifications will be presented in some rationalised form that gives them meaning and coherence. This is typically done by building a logical argument around some specific goal that is tied to some fundamental value[120] such as equality of opportunity, the primacy of human life, fairness, justice or well-being or by indirect reference to such values through more instrumental concepts such as professionalism, efficiency, effectiveness, good governance, profitability or value-for-money.

[120] A fundamental value is one that is presented as a universal principle not needing any justification.

Which rationalisations are selected, how they are presented, and what they mean, will be determined to a large extent by people's perceptions and dispositions. These, in turn, stem from the individual's underlying attitudes, interests and beliefs and in the context of a debate or some other discursive activity, they constitute what we are terming rationality criteria. Rationality criteria are the expressions of the deep-seated moral logic that underpin the individual's subjective judgements. They determine what the person understands to be "right" or "wrong", "ethical" or "unethical", "reasonable" or "unreasonable", and so on. The underlying rationality criteria upon which the rationalisations are founded will often normally remain unspoken and hidden from view. We can guess what attitudes and beliefs lie behind what is being said, but in normal communication we do not systematically expose our own, or seek to expose other people's values, prejudices and fundamental interests. We challenge other people's proposals but not the deep and unspoken values from which these proposals emerge. In this sense, most communication activities are 'surface' level and if, at the end of the meeting, we make a decision then our surface communication has produced a 'surface agreement'. Although little of our underlying attitudes have been expressed, we have still been able to negotiate a course of action by means of competitive argument.

Often two people will both make reference to the same value concept (e.g. 'fairness') or the same instrumental notion (e.g. 'efficiency'), but in using the term in the context of the discussion, each will have a somewhat different subjective understanding of what it means. A particular understanding of what 'fairness' or 'efficiency' means in a specific context is embedded in the values and attitudes (habitus) that give rise to the individual's rationality criteria. It is these criteria that predispose people to rationalise their arguments in one way rather than in some other way. You say your proposal is "fair" and I say that my proposal is "fair" - the trouble is, deep down, you and I do not mean quite the same thing by the word "fair". Even when it is non-disputed evidence that is being presented (rather than value statements), the evidence has to be filtered through personal perception as part of the discourse. As Carl Jung taught us, even when dealing with empirical data, we are necessarily speaking about ourselves.[121] Even when the debate centres on scientific facts and concrete evidence we should recognise that how those facts have been selected and presented will have been determined, in part at least, by personal attitudes and opinions.

As argued in chapter 6, in this situation two broad approaches towards deliberation activity present themselves. We could argue it out from the points of view of our different perspectives until, by some means, one of us 'wins' the argument and a decision is made. Alternatively, we could seek to reconcile our different meanings (in the context under consideration) and thereby generate a proposal that takes some account of both of our perspectives. A tendency towards the first approach produces what we are calling a surface agreement. A tendency towards the second approach produces what we are calling a deep agreement. A deep agreement involves the creation of meanings that are inter-subjectively understood. Inter-subjectivity exists when people in their interactions with each other construct shared meanings. Multiple rationality analysis seeks to provide an approach that will foster the emergence of such meanings. We might say that we are seeking to create a generative rather than a competitive discourse.

We communicate in all sorts of ways that transcend the word meanings of our statements. In 1950 the BBC began regular televised news bulletins. The newsreaders themselves were not seen on screen in case their facial expressions gave an indication of their personal opinions thereby compromising the Corporation's obligation to be impartial. Although in retrospect this policy seems over the top (and was soon abandoned), it is undoubtedly true that the things we do and the ways in which we do them can 'speak' volumes about what we think and believe. As we argued in chapter 1, in many instances, political and business honesty can be more readily perceived by what is done than by what is said. Even a spoken statement is a physical act and the dishonesty of what we are saying can be communicated by the way we say it. As Nietzsche put it, "One may sometimes tell a lie, but the grimace with which one accompanies it tells the truth." Furthermore, we all under-

[121] CW4 para 774).The Collected Works of C G Jung ed Herbert Read, Michael Fordam and Gerhard (Adler –n20 Vols. Routledge 1953-78).

stand that in argument we are not only influenced by words but also by what Samuel Butler termed "tone and temper".[122]

In spoken and written communication, we rationalise our arguments to give them practical meaning - how we rationalise depends on the interests, beliefs and values that underpin this practical meaning. Rationality analysts are concerned to provide an initial free-thinking dialogue that will allow each person involved in the subsequent decision discourse to become aware of his or her own and other people's rationality criteria. In this way, meanings become inter-subjectively understood and this, in turn, opens up the possibility of achieving creative rather than negotiated proposals for action. In competitive discourse one particular argument or proposal 'wins the day' - albeit in some form modified by acts of compromise and concession. By contrast, generative discourse produces ideas and proposals that none of the participants would have thought of on their own but which they now agree constitutes the most appropriate way forward. In generative discourse ideas are generated by the debate rather than positioned in the debate. In multiple rationality analysis (MRA) the objective is to move from competitive to generative discourse so as to achieve a 'deep' rather than a 'surface' agreement. For many decisions this is not necessary. For many other decisions it is necessary but does not happen – it is these that should be the focus of MRA.

We accept that people have different values and these are simply taken as a given. Whether we are having an argument down the pub or putting forward a point of view in a formal committee, we are not normally troubled by our intuitive awareness that beneath our own and other people's surface arguments and rationalisations lie webs of unspoken (and perhaps dimly understood) values and attitudes that are tied into an individual's fundamental beliefs, interests and agendas. Any attempt to bring these to the surface would normally be seen to be intellectually unnecessary, administratively expensive, procedurally strange or socially aggressive. Indeed, in most discursive situations there will be no wish or perceived need to analyse in a systematic fashion the underlying

[122] Anthropologist Ray Birdwhistell is accredited with pioneering the original study of non-verbal communication. He termed this work kinesics. Birdwhistell R.L. (1952), Introduction to Kinesics, University of Louisville Press.

rationality criteria being applied by the deliberators. Multiple rationality analysis is an approach to deliberation that need only be employed in situations where, like those pointed to above, it is agreed that a 'deep', rather than a 'surface', agreement is being sought. In particular, it is advocated as an approach to pre-planning those policies that are expected to have significant and irreversible, long-term impacts or where there is a recognised need to generate proposals that will be judged to be appropriate now and in the future by all those who have, or will have, some concrete interest or some emotional or value-stake in what happens. Before turning to the question of how to utilise this approach to strategic thinking and planning, we need to say a little more about the single biggest barrier to working in this way – ourselves.

The Principled Self

"In my relationships with persons I have found that it does not help, in the long run, to act as though I were something that I am not."
(Carl R. Rogers)

The emancipated self

To describe someone as 'authentic' suggests that they are the sort of person who means what they say and have the conscious intention to elevate substance over appearance and fact over opinion.[123] Simply put, authenticity is about 'integrity' and 'true motive'. Authentic individuals are free from self-deception: in this sense, they are 'emancipated'[124] and not held captive by their false beliefs and preconceptions. Buried somewhere in our psyches we all have an authentic self but it is only when we accept ourselves as we are that we can claim to be free from delusion and thus truly emancipated. The true, authentic self can be suppressed – we might almost say imprisoned - by ego (particularly when buried beneath an accumulation of social conditioning); but the truly emancipated self holds on to its authenticity by remaining aware of these limiting factors and being prepared to rise above them. For critical theorists, this somewhat philosophical point has important practical implications: it highlights the paradox that it is only by accepting ourselves as we are that we become able to learn and change.

To be authentic is to be intellectually emancipated and to be intellectually emancipated is to have the confidence to be open with others. It is this openness that is being sought in discussions based on 'ideal speech' principles. Under these conditions the expectation is – paradoxical as it might at first appear – that what is most personal and deeply felt in each of us is the very aspect that would, if it were to be shared and expressed, speak most deeply to others. Carl Rogers summarised this proposition neatly when

[123] In western philosophy, Kierkegaard is often associated with concerns about authenticity. Critical of the hypocrisy of organized religion, Kierkegaard distinguished 'authentic' Christianity from the structures and practices of Christendom.
[124] This is a term associated with the writings of Jurgen Habermas.

he suggested that "what is most personal is most general".[125] Before developing this idea, we need to emphasise that being 'emancipated' in this way is not the same thing as being 'principled'.

Consider the proposition:

"A life lived by principle leaves a person vulnerable to criticism".

Some of the real-world issues that are likely to come up in a discussion based on this proposition are well illustrated by the evangelical career of Richard R. Lyman.

> *"Principle, particularly moral principle, can never be a weathervane, spinning around this way and that with the shifting winds of expediency. Moral principle is a compass forever fixed and forever true."*
> *(Richard R. Lyman).*

Lyman served as an apostle of the Church of Jesus Christ of Latter Day Saints. He secretly embraced the Church's abandoned (1890) principle of plural marriage. The 1890 position had become banned under the new pronouncements of the Church's 1904 Second Manifesto. Although plural marriages performed between 1890 and 1904 were tolerated, his second marriage (1925) was deemed unacceptable and despite his prominent position in its hierarchy (perhaps because of it), he was excommunicated by the Church in 1943.

When personal principles clash with collective policy pronoucements, disputes within organisations are bound to emerge. To prevent institutional incoherence, religious communities, cabinet governments, political parties, boards of directors, charity trustees, and school governors all tend to embrace the rule of collective responsibility. This operational principle enables collective decisions to be made and implemented by groups that contain a variety of opinions and beliefs. Lyman's offence was that he acted in accordance with his personal morality and in so doing, he contravened the current policies of the church that he helped to lead.

[125] See discussion by Berkun at: Personal Insights on User / Professional Experience: Notes from a Multidisciplinary CSCW 1212 workshop. http://grumption.typepad.com/blog/2012/01/

THE NATURE OF PRINCIPLES

In earlier chapters we drew a distinction between universal (moral) and specific (pragmatic) principles. Following our discussions regarding the tensions between the ethical and the pragmatic, we will now consider some of the ways in which the notion of principle is employed by those charged with the responsibility for making policy decisions.

Often pragmatic principles are presented as fundamental values when in practice they are simply self-interested rules of engagement in a competitive discourse. Consider these two statements:

1. "What you're proposing has to be rejected because it is unprincipled."

2. "I understand that your point of view is sincerely held but I can't go along with your suggestion because it goes against my principles."

There is a subtle, but important, difference between the two underlying objections pointed to by these statements. On the face of it, they both seem to be arguing non-acceptance on the basis of an a priori principled (ethical) position. However, while the first clearly implies rejection on the basis of it contravening some form of universal moral value, the second is more equivocal; unlike the first, it could be interpreted as saying ' I accept that your position is principled – but my principles are different from yours'. Both universal and specific principles can be advanced in the rationalisation of an argument. The key difference between them, however, should be recognised. The tone and tenor of the second statement does not seem to rule out the possibility of a collaborative dialogue that could result in some degree of inter-subjective understanding. The first, on the other hand, openly declares an absolute unwillingness to seek any degree of shared agreement. The first would appear to lead inevitably to conflict and set up the conditions for a competitive discourse, while the second seems to leave open the possibility for creative, collaborative and generative dialogue. We can thus make a distinction between soft and hard principles. Hard principles are universal in nature, context free and cannot be modified through free and open discourse. They are, we might say, 'articles of faith' and are at the root of many a competitive discourse. Soft principles are specific in nature, tied to context and can sometimes be modified through generative discourse. They are, we might say, strongly held opinions rather than articles of faith.

To establish some initial structure to the process of rationality analysis, we can usefully make a distinction between (a) hard deep-seated principles that lead to essentially contested points of view; (b) soft pragmatic principled positions that can conceivably be reconciled through open debate; and (c) surface level misunderstandings that generate discursive concepts that can easily be reconciled through acts of clarification.

If a discourse is fractured by disagreements that are grounded in irreconcilable basic values or fundamental differences in belief systems, the communication is not so much distorted as 'locked'. An ideologically locked discourse occurs when a proposal is proffered or rejected on the grounds that it embraces or contravenes a universal value while, in reality, it is embedded in a local or personal set of self-serving attitudes: in other words, when what is unacceptable to me and my interests masquerades as being unconscionable. When this occurs, it takes the discussion into ideological territory. The common use of the word 'principle' to mean both a collection of ideological opinions and a generally accepted ethical value leads to communicative confusion.

> *"Ideology and communication more often than not run into each other than complement each other. Principle and communication work together. Ideology and communication often work apart."*
> *(Frank Luntz)[126]*

This communicative difficulty has to be addressed to avoid being unnecessarily locked into a competitive mode of argument. This is because it is virtually impossible to engage in policy discussions without making reference to 'principles'. A principle can be thought of as a generalised 'value wrapper' surrounding a number

[126] Frank Luntz is a US communications consultant who has advised many influential governmental and corporate organizations about the relationship between language use and effective strategy formation. This quotation has featured on his organization's website.

of specific judgements. In any open, generative discourse, a clear distinction has to be made between the use of the term 'principle' to mean the specific (personal/local) and the universal (cross-cultural).

NOTE

The relationship between the specific and the general goes to the heart of Immanuel Kant's ideas about the nature and scope of judgement. Kant made a distinction between "determinant" and "reflective" forms of judgement. He described judgement in general as the faculty of thinking the particular as contained within the universal and argued that if the universal is already given (a priori) then the judgement that contains the particular is "determinant". By contrast, if only the particular is asserted so that the general has to be deduced from it, then the judgement is regarded as "reflective". Unattached reflective judgements are, so to speak "in need of a principle" (a value 'wrapper') if they are to be tied into a general philosophical coherence. Kant's distinctions have a particular relevance to those seeking to analyse their own and other people's rationalisation of arguments because they ascribe two discretely different roles or aspects to the faculty of judgement: "determining" (bestimmend) and "reflecting" (relfektierend). The former justifies assertions by subsuming the particular under concepts (universals) that are already given. The latter seeks justifications through reasoned arguments that seek to "find" the universal for a given particular.

Rationality analysis is based on a belief in what Rorty terms "the virtues of curiosity, open-mindedness and conversability".[127] One of the operational propositions of this analysis is that the participants engaging in policy conversations have the potential to be aware of their own and each other's underlying interests and assumptions. As discussed elsewhere,[128] Anthony Giddens describes those who are capable of achieving this characteristic as being "knowledgeable actors".[129]

The Multi-Faceted Nature of Principles

In many policy debates, particularly in the political arena, practical, self-interested, proposals are presented as being founded on universal principles. "We should do this because it is the right thing

[127] *Op.cit. (1999) p.xxi.*

[128] *See Introduction and chapter 6.*

[129] *Giddens (1979) op.cit. See chapters 1 and 6 for discussion of knowledgeability.*

to do, not because it's in my interest." By being presented as being a universal principle and beyond pragmatism, the speaker seeks to stifle discussion. However, we have the capacity to understand a good deal about the nature of the circumstances surrounding a discourse and can often 'read' the politics of the situation. In the language of critical theory, we possess 'knowledgeability' and this psycho-social awareness provides the potential for us to distinguish between pragmatic reasoning (interest and context bound) and universal truth (pure reason or a genuine article of faith). It was Kant who taught us that it is motivation in context that determines whether or not an act is grounded in a universal moral principle. If lying is always wrong, then in Nazi Germany it would have been immoral to lie to the authorities regarding the whereabouts of a Jewish child who was hiding in an attic. If you lie to an armed burglar by denying that you keep money in the house, would that constitute an act of moral courage – or would it be a reprehensible dishonest thing to do?

Because all parties to a discourse are potentially knowledgeable, they have the capacity to be aware of their own and other people's cynical and hypocritical arguments. It is this capability that can lubricate open discourse and provide an opportunity to prevent a locking down of arguments. In other words, all is not lost when attempts are made to call upon the universality of a 'principle' to turn what might be a creative open debate about options into a predetermined, "self-evident", one-only conclusion. This is not to say that those holding to a strongly held political or religious position will necessarily loosen their ideological grip; to argue that would, of course, be naive. Nevertheless, the knowledgeability of actors does, in theory at least, make it conceivable that a locked discourse could be freed from the distortions of cynicism and hypocrisy (and thereby unlocked) if the arguments were to be revisited under ideal speech conditions.

Self knowledge that his or her position is really grounded in pragmatism or presumption rather than principle and reason, together with the awareness that the other actors understand this, can help shape the way in which an argument is presented and discussed. In particular, most people consciously or subconsciously make efforts to avoid appearing rigid, bigotted or over-principled.

It is this feature of human nature that provides an opportunity to set up and facilitate the discourse in a way that inhibits people from presenting instrumental values as though they are universal principles. The object of mulit-rational thinking is to allow all concerned to recognise a personal or local and instrumental value for what it is and, of course, for what it is not.[130] In policy discussions, where the notion of 'instrumental value' is substituted for that of 'universal principle', it signals that the actor concedes to the possibility of argument and that others may legitimately hold different values – and therefore different opinions. Another motivation for substituting the word 'value' for 'principle' in discursive situations is that the notion of 'principle' carries conotations of harshness and inflexibility while the idea of 'value' is somehow softer - emphasising decency and thoughtfulness rather than rigidity.[131] The *ideal* speech situation demanded by open multi-rational thinking, seeks to ensure that any pragmatic truth (or instrumental value) masquerading as a universal truth (or article of faith) is exposed.

All of this is rather theoretical and the reader who understands the distinctions being made here, might reasonably want to 'cut to the chase' and ask the more practical question, "How do we know that what is being referred to is a universal principle rather than a local pragmatic argument?"[132]

The transferability test

The clearest way of determining whether a statement is referencing a universal or a pragmatic principle is to employ the 'transferability test'. In the real world, pragmatism is a dominant feature of decision-making. In an exercise seeking to appraise how arguments are being rationalised (justified), the transferability test can be used as a device to clarify (expose) the contextual issues surrounding specific assertions. For a principle to have a

[130] See discussion on common sense in chapter 2 for amplification of this point.

[131] This idea of equating a person who pontificates about principles with someone who deserves criticism (or is even ripe for ridicule) is widely reinforced in classical western literature by a variety of novelists and playwrights including Jane Austin, Charles Dickens, Anton Chekhov, Gustav Flaubert and Leo Tolstoy (to mention but a few).

[132] Put more academically, this question might be reformulated as, "How is an ideal speech situation to be tested?"

universal application it must be shown to have the same moral and logical relevance in situations other than that in which it is currently being used. By contrast, a pragmatic principle might be seen to be relevant in the situation under consideration but not so relevant, or even irrelevant, in some other situation. A rather obvious example would be where an argument is proffered by a 'principled advocate' in favour of an anti-abortionist position by referencing the biblical commandment that "thou shalt not kill". If the sacredness of human life is argued for by someone as a basic value in the mega discourse surrounding abortion while, at the same time that person supports the death penalty and/or the taking up of arms in defense of the nation, they cannot claim the sacredness of human life to be a universal principle in support of their argument for outlawing abortion. This does not mean that their argument is unprincipled but rather that this particular prinicple is not universal (transferable) and thus its supposed comprehensiveness cannot be called upon as a rationale for outlawing abortion. A full and inter-subjective understanding (knowledgeability) of the role that context plays in principled assertions can be the key to opening a locked discourse. Understanding oneself lies at the heart of this unlocking.

The idea of 'transferability' is analogous to the notion of 'universality' as considered by writers such as Noam Chomsky and Basil Bernstein. Chomsky's "principle of universality" argues that we should apply to ourselves the same ethical standards that we apply to others. He argues that evolution seems to have implanted in all of us an egotistical tendency to be less judgemental of our own behaviour than we are of others' and that this can result in the egocentric assumption that our values ARE universal.

THE 'AUTHENTIC SELF'

In 1956 Carl R. Rogers first published his now often-quoted paradoxical remark that "what is most personal is most universal".[133] In the second half of the twentieth century, Rogers outlined what was then a radical approach to counselling and therapy that shifted the emphasis away from a reliance on technique and the assumed authority of the qualified therapist, to one that emphasised the

[133] The 1956 essay 'This is Me': The Development of My Professional Thinking and Personal Philosophy' that was reprinted in chapter 1 of his influential book On Becoming a Person: A Therapist's View of Psychotherapy (1961) First published in the UK by Constable & Robinson (London: 1967) and constantly quoted on subsequent works on psychotherapy.

importance of the therapeutic relationship. The subsequent development of the now highly influential client-centred approach to counselling has played a part in providing an offically recognised (accredited) acceptance of the value of personal experiences and interpretations in the practice of psychiatry. From its source in psycho-philosophy, it has spread to influence other practices such as student-centred learning, user-centred design and customer-focused business strategies.

To be clear, Rogers' famous quote was not meant to imply that what he understood from his experiences was necessarily true for other people: he was making a subtler and more significant point about the need (in therapeutic relationships) for practitioners to be themselves. He described as a "curious paradox" the fact that when he, "a decidedly imperfect person", accepted himself as he was, his relationships with clients deepened and hoped-for professional outcomes were more readily achieved.

Probably a more popular and better-known quotation than that of Rogers' is the cynical saying that "the secret of success is sincerity: fake that and you've got it made."[134] The faking of sincerity is an essential part of the armoury of successful actors, politicians and (some would say) business people. In the case of actors this skill is clearly to be admired – but what about politicians and business people? When duplicitous decision-makers take on an 'act' and attempt to influence others by presenting themselves as frank, honest people, free from guile and just themselves, we are presented with what is arguably the greatest of all personal deceits – someone pretending to be what they are not. When someone says about themselves that "what you see is what you get" it seldom means that they have become self-aware. More often than not, it is an indication that they want to be regarded as a down-to-earth, straight-talking individual. There is, of course, a great deal of difference between wanting to be regarded as sincere and authentically being sincere.

Douglas Murray makes the point that the rise of the internet has brought with it some fudging of the distinction between private

[134] This jokey observation (or versions of it) has been attributed to a number of different sources including Anonymous, Samuel Goldwyn, Groucho Marx, and George Burns.

and public debate. There was a time, not so long ago, that people would express their thoughts in private settings in ways that they would not dream of doing in public settings. Quick off-the-cuff comments on public affairs to friends and family would be couched in a different language to that used in formal settings. In informal social settings our language was (and of course largely still is) designed to engage and entertain rather than purposively argue for a course of action with an expectation that it will call forth some corporate, local or national response. In contrast, in public decision-making forums, our utterances tend to be more measured and thought through: if we are part of a decision-making group we recognize that how we express our opinions has a strategic significance that has to be taken into account. The impact of what we say in public and how we say it can have political consequences that do not exist in informal social situations. Although in professional and political settings an effort would normally be made to engage in some pre-thinking and research before pontificating, in closed social settings we are much more likely to express our thoughts in a crude, off-the-cuff fashion, exaggerating and colouring our views in order to stimulate the 'game' of social argument (that after all will have no practical consequences in the real world of affairs).

In the age of the internet, such platforms as emails, Facebook, Tweets and Instagrams have provided millions of us (including the powerful and influential) with a place to pontificate off-the-cuff. In this way, it is possible for a chief executive, president, prime minister or other powerful individual to share with the world at large his or her ill-considered thoughts that once would be rehearsed in private. A Tweet has the characteristics of the 'private' whilst being, in effect, distinctly public in nature: this is true whether it is posted from a teenager's bedroom or the Oval Office of the White House.

Internet exchanges do not take place face-to-face and are often consciously shaped by fabrications, carefully selected images such as edited photographs, mock-ups or other forms of artifice such as fake news and conspiracy theories. A manufactured self-image takes precedence over the presentation of authentic self and, more significantly, polarized simplistic arguments displace considered points of view. In short, the internet has a tendency to heighten competitive discourse and inhibit attempts to shift a policy discussion towards a more generative approach.

These sympathetically distorted pictures of who we are have become part of the fabric of how we engage on line. Andrew Potter, author of The Authenticity Hoax, considered the problems that arise when we feel in one way but choose to perform in another. In the modern world our natural feelings get contorted in various ways in order to conform to what institutions demand and conventions expect. Most days, simply to get along, we have to put on a false face and fake our publicly expressed emotions. Potter suggests that, realistically, our best hope of being 'authentic' is to bring the two aspects of who we are into alignment – our true feelings and beliefs and what we say we feel and believe. He sees modern authenticity as the capacity to live comfortably with the natural self we really are and the manufactured persona we present to the world. Contemporary forms of communication have embraced – some would say intensified – the duality of the 'two selves'. Social media platforms do not so much portray who we are, as provide insights into what we want others to believe we are. To survive in the modern world of social affairs, acting is inevitable and the authentic self is not so much someone who behaves in a completely uninhibited fashion, as someone who is aware of both how and why the distorted self is presented to others. In this sense, authenticity is an aspect of knowledgeability. The social value of authenticity is that it brings with it assumptions about self-respect and trustworthiness. Herein lies its significance to decision-making. A group of policy-makers who are aware (knowledgeable) of their own and each other's masks, have an opportunity to act more authentically and in so doing make more genuinely sustainable decisions.

Postscript

From Theory to Practice

"There is no war between theory and practice."
(Charles Kettering)

In these essays I have focused on theory. In particular, I have considered how philosophy and social critical theory can provide insights into why and how decision discourses become distorted and thereby lead to regrettable actions and flawed policies. Although, at times, I have pointed to practical implications of the analysis,[135] I have not sought to provide a 'how to' manual for generative discourse. Those wishing to incorporate rationality analysis into their strategic thinking must work out for themselves how best this might be achieved given the nature of the particular decision they are considering. I will, however, conclude by making some general suggestions about how to go about the shift from theory to practice. Let's begin by pointing to some accessible follow-up reading that will help those wishing to operationalize the ideas we have discussed.

- Additional support materials can be found in the MRA section of the following website: leapingfrogpublications.co.uk. This site provides some MRA case studies. It also provides a place for sharing ideas and is constantly updated.
- Appendix 2 (below) provides a starting point for those readers wishing to dig deeper into the relationship between multiple rationality analysis and strategic thinking. It focuses on the difference between strategic thinking and strategic planning.
- Appendix 1 (below) considers the importance of multi-rational thinking for commercial enterprises wishing to be successful in the changing political climate of the twenty-first century.
- In their recent book, Peter Osborn and Eddy Canfor-Dumas outline some useful techniques that can be applied during the operation of a multi-rational discussion. [The Talking Revolution: How Creative Conversation Can Change the World, Port Meadow Press (2018). Chapter 4 is particularly interesting and relevant].

[135] See in particular end of chapter 6.

FINAL COMMENTS

The modus operandi of a sustainable decision-making event is itself context driven: there is no one definitive way of 'doing' an open discourse. The minimum agreement, so to speak, is for all concerned to commit to engaging in free and uninhibited debate that consciously seeks to operate within a creative rather than a competitive atmosphere. This involves agreeing to the systematic analysis of justifications rather than mindlessly arguing over pre-prepared concrete proposals. Beyond this commitment to pursue an ideal speech situation, there is no prescribed method for seeking 'sustainable' outcomes from policy discussions.[136] Although the application of multiple rationality thinking and analysis to decision-making requires this minimum commitment, the operational arrangements do not need to be onerous or difficult. In its simplest conception it can be regarded as a pre-decision exercise designed to get all the parties to recognize the benefits that can be derived from taking a generative approach to decision-making.

Fig.1

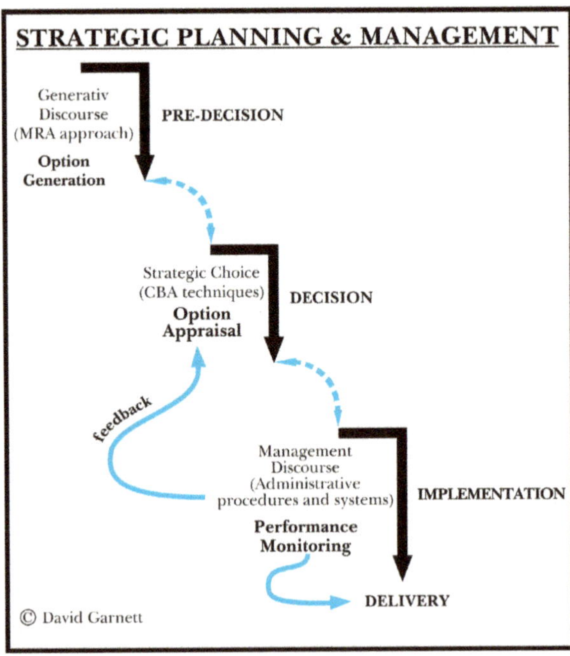

[136] See the Introduction and Chapter 1 for discussion of the meaning of "sustainable" in this context.

The preplanning period of analytical thinking is designed to set overarching value priorities and generate options based on a shared understanding of the meanings that people place on disputed concepts. It seeks to generate a 'deep agreement' of who constitutes the stakeholders in a decision and also makes explicit the nature of each of their stakes - together with the various stakeholders' underlying personal assumptions, attitudes and predispositions. In this context the term 'decision' refers to the process of option appraisal and selection while the term 'pre-decision' refers to this prior process of deliberation that clarifies the subjective value and overt interest contexts within which the cost-benefit-analysis occurs. The one seeks to choose between options while the other is concerned with the prior activity of generating the appropriate range of options to be appraised. Multiple rationality analysis is not the same thing as option appraisal. The focus of the former is on rational justifications and ethical practices while the focus of the latter is on economic analysis and measurement. As decision tools they are not mutually exclusive but rather, they work in tandem to produce sustainable decisions.

Multiple rationality analysis requires the establishment of a decision procedure that moves from a generative discourse (thinking) to a strategic plan (choosing), to implementation (acting), and then to systems that feed back into strategic thinking and planning (managing and monitoring).

What are 'multiple rationalities' and why analyse them?

In these essays I have made the point that historically, philosophy has not so much been concerned with the search for 'truth' as investigating the nature of 'truth'. We have concluded that in certain contexts 'truth' is a relative concept. For decision-makers this presents a problem. If social reality is embedded in a multiplicity of perspectives, then social policy-making should be regarded as an interdisciplinary, thought-provoking exercise.

The book's interdisciplinary approach makes it a key text for anyone concerned with the successful operation of complex social issues or where service provision operates through some form of interagency working. Successful interagency working requires the coming together of different professional cultures to solve complex social problems. The recent growth of interagency working is being intensified by the rapid introduction of the 'joint commissioning' model of service provision. Our argument has been that no one perspective on the world can encapsulate all the intricate issues that need to be considered when seeking to make sustainable social policy decisions. Indeed, we should be very wary indeed of anyone who thinks that we can capture everything that is 'true' about a social issue from one perspective.

generating the 'yet-to-be-thought'

While it is inevitable that decision-makers will have preconceived opinions, it is important that these views do not unnecessarily restrict the creativity of their thinking, the objectivity of their analysis or the ability to see someone else's point of view. Multiple rationality analysis seeks to achieve this 'emancipated' position by establishing an element of self-awareness into the decision-making process. This means that it is more than a simple brainstorming technique: it is a commitment to try to consider the issue being considered in a way that is free from bias and ideological preconceptions. It is, in other words, a sort of contract to engage in what we might term emancipated judgement.[137]

Other types of 'open' meeting such as citizens' panels, focus groups and opinion surveys are often employed as precursors to decision-making. The main point, however, is that such techniques, including typical brainstorming exercises, do not overcome those discursive distortions that stem from the predispositions of those participating in the exercise. A traditional brainstorming exercise produces a range of options that are then considered in a largely competitive discourse. By contrast, multiple rationality analysis seeks to emancipate thought from cultural constraints rather than simply encourage freedom of thought within an established cultural framework. In this way it provides the context for a creative discourse capable of generating the 'yet-to-be-thought'. Although organised as open sessions, typical brainstorming exercises still operate within a framework of established power relations that are the essential constraining features of a 'distorted communica-

[137] An idea related to Habermas' notion of 'emancipated thought' that is a precondition of an ideal speech situation (see chapter 5).

tion'. In these essays I have argued that this need not be the case and that it is possible to interact in ways that embrace the emancipatory principles of rationality analysis.

Is MRA a technique?

It is not a technique but an attitude to strategic thinking: it can be thought of as a set of operational guidelines. These guidelines provide the principles that set in place the approach to subsequent decision meetings. MRA is largely a way of discussing and arguing. It is a mind-set rather than a manual and it is more cultural than technical. Each decision group or policy committee needs to agree its own rules of discourse. These will vary according to circumstances but must be established at the outset.

Where initial opinions clash and proposed courses of action differ, these have to be confronted as part of the pre-planning discourse. This might simply involve an open discussion chaired by an independent facilitator who identifies and records points of conflict. In some cases it might be appropriate to devise a formal exercise as a way of stimulating the discussion. One of the simplest I have used involves requiring participants to list the three best (most valid) points in their opponents' argument. Where 'principles' clash, disagreement is likely to be fundamental. The transferability test (chapter 6) can sometimes be used as a way of opening up the discussion when it becomes blocked by 'principled' disagreements.

Multiple rationality analysis was developed by the author in the 1990s as part of a research project into the nature and scope of intergenerational justice. [Garnett D. 'Absent Voices: Accommodating the Interests of Future Generations in Current Decision-Making Processes', in a paper presented to the Second International Conference of the European Society for Ecological Economics, University of Geneva, March 1998. Revised and reprinted as 'Absent Voices: Accommodating the Interests of Future Generations Through Multiple Rationality Analysis, in the International Journal of Sustainable Development, Vol. 2, No.4.in].

Practitioners who have tried unsuccessfully to put ideas into practice sometimes make the point that "in theory, theory and practice are the same - but in practice, they are not".[138] Like the

[138] *Attributed to Albert Einstein.*

sayings of Donald Rumsfeld, this observation opaquely captures some sort of truth about social and political life. In the field of social affairs, writers often wrongly assume that so long as they are clearly expressed, the practical application of ideas is unproblematic. In reality, the clear articulation of theory does not necessarily guarantee a basis for effective practical application. In this case, however, the hope is that the arguments laid out in these essays are compelling and clear enough to spark off in the reader's mind thoughts about how to improve the quality of important decision discourses. Whether this is the case or not, why not keep in touch.

www.leapingfrogpublications.co.uk

Shared Value

"Shareholder value should be a result not an objective."

Until recently there was a generally held belief that company executives have an over-riding duty to maximise shareholder value (see chapter 1). This idea became entrenched in business attitudes in the last quarter of the twentieth century. It is still sometimes referred to as a sort of 'moral responsibility'. Until recently, this persistent attitude acted as a barrier to the introduction of socially orientated business cultures. Things are changing.

The global financial crunch of 2008 was a severe worldwide economic disaster considered by many economists to have been the most serious financial crisis since the Great Depression of the 1930s, to which it is often compared. Among other things, the turmoil brought about a reassessment of the relationship between business and community interests. This debate about the responsibilities of the business community has since been stimulated by other concerns. Many now argue that the world is facing a climate catastrophe and businesses around the world must address it urgently or face the ultimate sanction for a public company - shareholders who refuse to back them any more. It is worth noting that this is not a message from an environmental action group but from the largest money manager in the UK, Legal & General Investment Management, which manages £1 trillion worth of UK pension fund investments: global warming was the top of its list of concerns about the way companies are run. Other red lights signalled by the fund managers included the level of executive pay, lack of diversity in senior corporate roles, the nature (and cost) of political lobbying and the poor quality of the financial information provided by auditors.

New consumer pressures are also impacting on corporate thinking and planning. A case in point is the major car manufacturers that are rapidly moving into electric vehicle production - not so much because they see it as an obvious extension of their established business models that will generate quick and easy profits - but rather because their future credibility will depend on being seen to be responding to societal pressure to participate in tackling environmental concerns.

What is taking place is much more significant than simple (cynical) virtue signalling. There is an emerging argument, increasingly accepted by business itself, that in the twenty-first century the commercial success of an individual company will depend, to a large extent, on it being seen to be responding to community and global concerns. Put simply, the business argument has shifted and many are now arguing that to be successful, a company has to be seen to be sharing the value it creates with the community as well as with its shareholders. This emerging phenomenon is referred to as 'shared value philosophy'.

What Is 'Shared Value'?

> *"We believe that the idea of shared value will give rise to the next major transformation of business thinking."*
> *(The Harvard Business School)*

In its simplest form 'shared value philosophy' can be thought of as a rational belief that the long-term success of any company depends on the health and wellbeing of its employees, customers, and the communities in which it operates. According to the Harvard Business School, shared value is the 'big idea' for business success in the twenty-first century. It advocates corporate policies and practices that enhance the competitive advantage and profitability of a company whilst simultaneously advancing social and economic conditions in the communities in which it operates.

The shared value approach is based on research findings that indicate that profit-seeking companies have much to gain by embracing more than simply shareholder interests. It also indicates that social and public enterprises, such as medical services, local authorities, police forces, schools, universities, and housing agencies, can embrace shared value philosophy in ways that enhance coherence and meaning to their changing role in modern society.

A number of highly successful profit-orientated companies such as GE, Google, IBM, Intel, Johnson & Johnson, Nestlé, Unilever, and Wal-Mart have recently modified their business models in ways that incorporate a shared value approach to their operations. Large and important companies are taking the lead and embracing the idea of shared value as a way of strengthening their identities and clarifying their roles as modern businesses.

The best of all monopoly profits . . .

Shared value is not so much a new idea as the latest manifestation of a long-standing concern to develop an appropriate relationship between business and society: that is, a relationship that takes account of more than crude market forces. As well as Christian principles, the paternalistic benevolence of nineteenth century industrial philanthropists such as George Peabody, Titus Salt and George and Richard Cadbury reflected an underlying commitment to ethical capitalism. Among other things, progressive entrepreneurs pointed to the tangible benefits to the firm of sharing the rewards of business output with the workforce - an idea that was famously demonstrated by Robert Owen's application of the notion of 'the economy of high wages'. By the middle of the twentieth century economists had incorporated a theory of 'commercial self interest' into the analysis of why monopoly power should be controlled. This idea was succinctly summarised by John Hick's often quoted observation that "The best of all monopoly profits is a quiet life." (Professor Sir John Hicks 1935).

Shared Value is not the same thing as Corporate Social Responsibility

By the last quarter of the twentieth century, a number of firms were declaring a commitment to 'corporate social responsibility' (CSR). This can be thought of as an approach to business that actively seeks to make a positive contribution to society. In practice the term can refer to a wide range of actions that companies may take, from donating to charity to reducing carbon emissions. The Harvard Business School approach argues for the efficacy of instigating more fundamental changes in business thinking and suggests that in the political and commercial climate following the financial crises of the late 1980s and early 1990s, successful companies need to review their relationships with society in a more fundamental way. The criticism of CSR is that it does not represent a full cultural commitment to being a valued part of society but rather it maintains an "old-fashioned" (and increasingly inappropriate) view of nineteenth and twentieth century benevolent capitalism. Social organisations and government entities often see success solely in terms of the external (e.g. community) benefits achieved or the money expended. By failing to embed the creation of social value into the business plan, the advocates of shared value argue that the 'good works' of the corporately responsible firm are little more than 'bolt-ons' to their traditional ways of working.

The concept of shared value involves the declaration of a social dividend as an integral part of an organisation's business practices. This approach moves away from a business model in which the firm donates a small proportion of its distributable profits to 'good causes', to one in which proper recognition is given to the fact that the firm is part of the community in which it operates. By engaging directly with wider concerns, the organisation strengthens its position in the community and this in turn enhances its competitiveness and creates a variety of productivity benefits.

Fig.1 'Shared Value': An Emerging Idea

Its advocates make the point that shared value is not the same thing as corporate social responsibility (CSR), philanthropy, or

even sustainability: it is, they suggest, a new business model appropriate for the demands of the twenty-first century. They see it as a radical development of the preceding models of ethical capitalism and argue that it more fully meets the challenges of our times.
In recent years, business policies have been regarded by many as a major cause of current social, environmental and economic

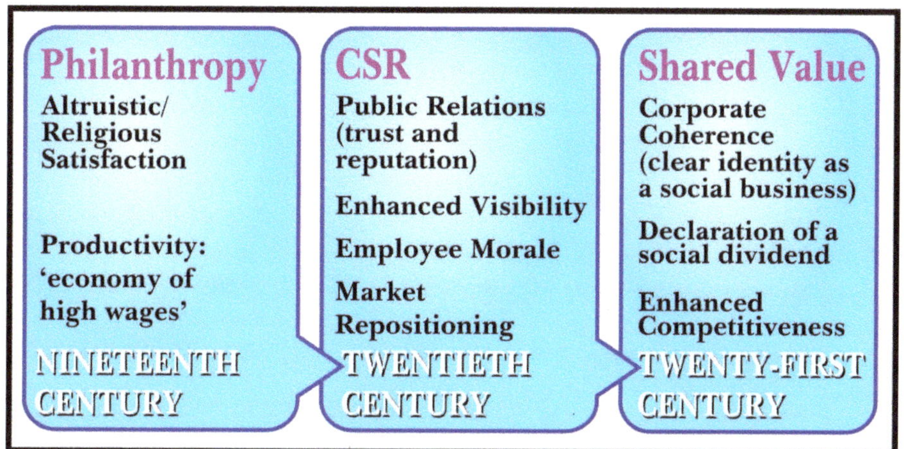

Fig.2 An Emerging Business Model

problems. Some companies are perceived to be prospering at the expense of the wider community. There is even a danger that the more business has begun to embrace corporate responsibility, the more it has been blamed for society's failures. The legitimacy of business practices is being challenged and the respect for areas of business such as banking and financial services has fallen to levels not seen in recent history.

The diminished trust in business has led political leaders to introduce regulatory arrangements that could undermine the flexibility and freedom of business decision-making and thereby inhibit economic growth and innovation. The proponents of shared value suggest that much of the problem lies with companies themselves, which they see as being locked into business models that are no longer adequate to the needs and expectations of modern society. The adoption of a shared value model provides an opportunity for an organisation to contribute to the wellbeing of society whilst stealing a march on its competitors.

Strategic Thinking

"Our opinions become fixed at the point where we stop thinking".
(Ernest Renan)

The meaning of strategy

Much confusion now surrounds the meaning of the term "strategy". Indeed, we might agree with the sentiment that "strategy has become a catchall term used to mean whatever one wants it to mean".[139] The current tendency to use the term 'strategy' when what is really meant is 'action plans' is more than a pedantic point of semantic concern: the inappropriate use of the term undermines the capacity of some organisations to establish a coherent approach to the management and development of their business interests.

'Strategy' is a term derived from the military lexicon. The word itself comes from the Greek strategia, meaning "generalship." In the military context, it is used to distinguish the role of the General Staff from that of lower ranked officers. It is the strategy that sets the overall battle plan while the hour-by-hour battlefield decisions are directed by the 'tactics' of the more junior field commanders. The battle strategy typically involves campaign planning and the deploying of troops and equipment into position prior to the battle. Once the battle starts, attention shifts from strategy to tactics. If we substitute "resources" for troops and equipment, "CEOs and directors or ministers" for generals and chiefs of staff, "middle managers, team leaders and civil servants" for field officers, and "management" for tactics - the transfer of the concept into the business and political worlds begins to take shape.

In the early management literature on the subject an organisation's strategy tended to be treated as a kind of campaign plan operating in the battlefield of the commercial marketplace. It first appeared in management literature in the second half of the twentieth century as a way of describing those company plans and actions that are designed to out-manoeuvre competitors. By 1980 influential

[139] Hambrick and Fredrickson, 'Are you sure you have a strategy?' In the Academy of Management Executive (2001), Vol.15, No.4.

writers such as George Steiner had popularised the idea of strategic planning and it had become a prominent element in the business management curricula of most business schools. It was from this time that the term began to be used to describe a whole range of policy elements so that both academics and practitioners began referring to an organization's 'pricing strategy', 'purchasing strategy', 'public relations strategy', 'borrowing strategy', etc. This tendency to apply the term to component policy elements had the effect of confusing and fudging the distinction between the firm's long-term overarching corporate mission and the various shorter-term action plans that come together to deliver the aims and associated outcomes of this business intent. In the mid 1990s, Henry Mintzberg famously commented on the increasingly confusing use of the term in his influential book The Rise and Fall of Strategic Planning.[140]

Mintzberg argued that the notion of 'strategy' had come to mean discretely different things in different contexts. Using a range of real life examples he illustrated the various ways in which the term had become unhelpfully confusing. This confusion clearly persists. It is, for example, commonly used to mean a plan - as in a 'strategy' of how to get from where we are to where we want to be. It is also sometimes used to describe an organization's operating perspective (vision). In this use it outlines an organization's broad approach to business - that is, its highly generalised objective to maximise profits, heal the sick, improve the living conditions of the poor, or demonstrate corporate social responsibility etc. In recent years, it has also been used to describe organizations' various approaches to marketing. A company that focuses on supplying relatively expensive goods or services to wealthier customers and clients, for example, is sometimes said to be pursuing a 'high end marketing strategy'. Similarly, a business that arranges fixed interest charges on part of its long-term debt might describe the action as part of its 'funding strategy'; or a legal firm that provides pro bono services to poorer people in the community might regard this non-profitable work as part of its 'public relations strategy'.

Despite the efforts of Mintzberg and others[141] to bring both clarity

[140] Mintzberg H (1994), Prentice Hall.

[141] Notably Kenneth Andrews, Michael Porter, Michel Robert, Michael Treacy and Fred Wiersema.

and usefulness to the concept by emphasising the crucial importance of seeing corporate strategy as the coordination of action plans for a purpose (rather than attaching the word to the plans themselves), the term is still constantly applied to the fragmented elements of business planning and management. And this remains a problem.

> *"When executives call everything strategy, and end up with a collection of strategies, they create confusion and undermine their own credibility. They especially reveal that they don't really have an integrated conception of the business."*
> *(Hambrick and Fredrickson, op. cit. p.49.)*

In seeking to clarify the meaning of strategy in a business context, Hambrick and Fredrickson (and others who might be regarded as belonging to the Mintzberg School of Thought) suggest that it should not be confused with an organization's mission, values and corporate objectives; nor should it be applied to its marketing or other tangible action plans (see fig.1). The corporate strategy represents the pattern of choices that reveals its underlying values, determines its objectives and produces the policies and plans for achieving those objectives. It is at this higher level of strategic thinking that decision-makers need to apply the principles of multiple rationality analysis. Indeed, we would argue that a failure to commit to rationality analysis as part of the process of complex decision-making makes effective high level strategic thinking impossible.

In what follows, for the sake of clarity, the idea of strategy will focus on corporate entities. This will require some linguistic shift into 'management speak'. Behind the argument, however, lies MRA's philosophical commitment to make explicit any intentional biases or attempts to distort the decision discourse in ways that support sectional interests.

To get started we will lay out (albeit rather crudely) how the standard management literature views the nature and scope of institutional strategy. The following postulated schema outlines some of the similarities and differences between a corporate and a political strategy.

The assumed key features of a sound corporate strategy

- It is a discourse in which important business choices are made.
- It is steered and constrained by the organization's mission and values.
- It is informed by objective research and analysis about the future and by the rationally analysed experiences of the present and past.
- It emerges over time and is continually adapted as assumptions and intentions collide with a changing reality: it is an evolving view of what is required to obtain long-run business success.
- It is about the deployment of limited resources for the attainment of ends.
- It articulates the organization's high-level goals not so much by specifying what they are as by specifying how they are to be achieved.
- It is the joint province of those who govern and those who manage.
- It positions the business in its operating market(s) and establishes a corporate perspective (identity) that differentiates it from its competitors and partners.
- It creates a coherent approach to the business's operational activities and seeks to coordinate those activities purposively.

The key features of a sound political strategy

- It is an open discourse in which important political choices are made.
- It is about the deployment of limited resources for the attainment of coherent ends.
- It is steered and constrained by the administration's legal powers, responsibilities and manifesto promises.
- It balances ethical views about the nature of long-term social justice with the pragmatics of current political and economic expediency.
- It is open to scrutiny by constituents and stakeholders.
- It is informed by objective research and analysis.
- It articulates the authority's socio-political goals not only by specifying what they are but also by how they are to be achieved.
- It is flexible and allows for post enactment adaptations if

circumstances change or initial assumptions collide with operational experience.

- It is informed by the knowledge, experience and expertise of appointed managers, officers and civil servants.
- It is the ultimate responsibility of elected members.
- It creates a coherent approach to the authority's operational activities and seeks to coordinate those activities purposively.

The primary objective of a strategy is to give the organization a sense of long-term purpose and a clear overall corporate coherence. To have practical effect, the strategy's coherence must not only be thought through, but it must also be communicated to, and understood by, all those whose decisions have an impact on the business. In order to communicate its logic to those directing and managing the organization, the strategy discourse must be capable of being analysed in a clear and systematic fashion. What is not always recognized, however, is that for it to be sustainable, it must be capable of reconciling the legitimate interests of all current and future stakeholders. This means that fully effective analysis requires an inter-subjective understanding of contested concepts and an appreciation of other people's views. To put it another way, effective strategic thinking requires the accommodation of both competing and complementary rationalities.

Orchestrating the strategy

Elsewhere in this text we have made the point that in our philosophy of social affairs the pursuit of truth has no substantive meaning and should be abandoned for the pursuit of best practice. 'Truth', we might say, is relative to discourse: change the nature of the discourse and we change what gets counted as 'best practice'. Addressing the issue of strategic management practice, takes us back to the question of 'generalship'. Ministers, top civil servants, boards of management and senior executives have the over-arching 'general' responsibility for orchestrating the organization's activities in ways that create operational coherence through time. We must not forget, however, that although coherence is a necessary, it is not a sufficient, criterion for the realisation of a sound strategy. A strategy can be coherent but misguided - a strategy needs to be successful as well as coherent. What constitutes 'success' in this context, and how to quantify it, brings to the fore practical issues that are addressed by employing the appropriate appraisal tools identified in the management practice literature.[142] The point being made here is that the strategic discourse is not the same thing as the policy planning process - rather it is the ***discursive framework within which intentional, informed and integrated choices are made.*** In short we can say that whether corporate or political, a sustainable strategy takes the form of a generative discourse that precedes the activity of strategic planning. We will now consider the nature and scope of strategic thinking and why it is not the same thing as strategic planning.

BECOMING STRATEGIC: THINKING

In decision-making, the relationship between theory and practice is mirrored by the relationship between thinking and planning. In the business management literature strategic thinking and strategic planning are not always clearly differentiated. If, however, we are concerned to make sustainable decisions, strategic thinking and strategic planning must be treated as distinct procedures.

Loizos Heracleos (1998) makes the point that effective decision-making can only occur when strategic thinking and strategic planning are interrelated in a dialectical process. In other words, each is a necessary but not sufficient requirement for the creation of sound policies. Planning a strategy without thinking about its purpose is a bit like designing a building without considering its function.[143]

In effective policy-making there needs to be an interactive thought process of divergence and convergence: being theoretical and then practical – being idealistic and then pragmatic - being strategic and then tactical - being synthetic but also analytical – understanding the present and then envisioning possible futures – in short: thinking and THEN planning. As the Mexican poet Octavio Paz put it, "Wisdom neither lies in fixity nor in change, but in the dialectic between the two".

Jeanne Leidtka (1998) makes the same point about the dialectical nature of sound strategic thinking: she describes the process

[142] These tend to take some form of cost-benefit appraisal: the description of which is beyond the scope of this text.

[143] As Louis Sullivan famously said about architecture: "forms follows function".

as being one of disruption and realignment. The suggestion here is that an appropriately broad view of the strategy-making process should incorporate both strategic thinking and strategic programming and regard them as related activities. This simple model (see fig.1 below) portrays the making of strategy as a continuous process of creation, disruption and realignment between an organization's present goals and obligations and its future needs and objectives.

Leidtka points out that both academics and practitioners have embraced the McKinsey "7S Model" that aligns strategy, structure, systems, superordinate goals, staff, skills, and shared values. The model has become influential and most modern managers recognise that purposeful, efficient organisational action cannot be taken if these "S" factors work at cross-purposes. Ironically, however, once aligned, these factors become a powerful impediment to change and the pursuit of continuous improvement. This is because the alignment establishes a culture of operational inertia – "If it's working don't change it". Indeed, it is clearly true that unnecessary change is costly and distracting and change for change's sake is not an intelligent management strategy.

The notion that 'newer is truer' clearly cannot be taken as a universal principle of political or corporate life. However, the learning organisation will develop a capacity to adapt and incorporate flexibility and opportunism into its operations by aligning the 7Ss in an appropriate (and temporary) fashion. The dilemma is that unaligned, these factors work at cross-purposes - aligned they drive out potentially needed change. Therefore we have to accept that for the progressive organisation that achieves 'continuous improvement' (social sector) or stays ahead of its competitors (commercial sector), the alignment is necessarily unstable. This in turn, implies the need to engage in strategic thinking as a continuous process rather than a periodic activity.

The cultural framework within which strategy is formulated needs to be constituted in ways that encourage the continuous examination of the tensions that always exist between, on the one hand, the creation of the alignment necessary to support efficiency and effectiveness and on the other hand, the disruption of alignment necessary to foster change and adaptability. Strategic thinking at its best disrupts alignment by creating a gap in the minds of managers between today's reality and a more desirable future. This, in turn, motivates the organisation to challenge the current strategy and its associated corporate plan. It should bring about a new (or modified) strategic intent. Translating the reformulated strategic intent into new institutional behaviours however, necessitates strategic programming (i.e. the realignment of structures, systems, processes, and skills around the new intent in a way that begins to close the gap that strategic thinking opened). Once closed, a new gap is opened in an iterative and continuous cycle of strategic thinking and strategic programming. The idea of this broadened view of the strategy-making process is captured in Figure 1.

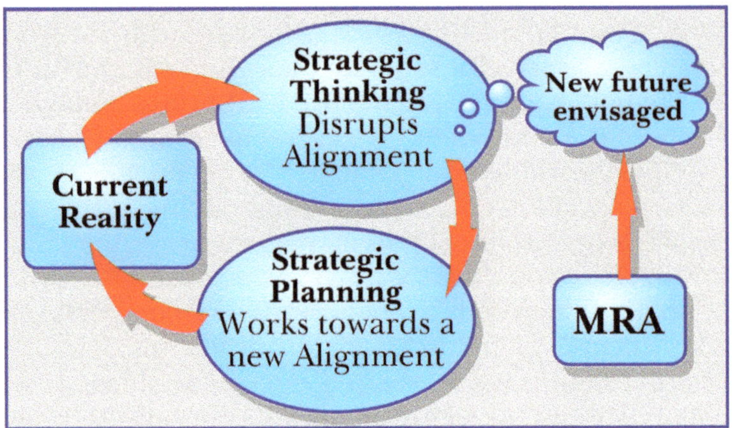

Figure 1: Strategy Making as a Dialectic

Fig.1 postulates the need for some form of multiple rationality analysis to be incorporated into the processes of strategic thinking and risk management. Before considering the nature and scope of strategic thinking (as against strategic planning), we can summarise the argument so far:

> *"It all comes down to the ability to go up and down the ladder of abstraction, and being able to see both the big picture and the operational implications, which are signs of outstanding leaders and strategists." (Heracleos 1998)*

How to think strategically

The need for successful strategies to be fully thought out before making plans for their implementation seems to be an uncontroversial observation. Indeed, it is inevitably the case that in all effective organizations, strategic plans stem from strategic judgements that have been thought through and argued for in an open way at the highest levels of governance and management. However, this leaves open three key questions that often lack clear answers. First, 'What is the nature of strategic thinking? Second, 'What are its parameters, and what is its relationship to strategic planning?' Third, 'What part do those outside of managing committees, cabinets, boards and executive groups have in the process of strategic thinking?' By focusing on the first two of these questions, we automatically address the third.

The importance of strategic thinking is continuously emphasised in the literature on strategic management. However, as argued above, the lack of a clear articulation as to the nature of this concept has lead to a degree of confusion. For example, strategic thinking has been presented as a somewhat higher order of strategic planning; as an alternative to strategic planning; and as an approach that is downright incompatible with strategic planning. Inadequate delineation of the precise characteristics of strategic thinking has also impeded its implementation by practitioners and its further development by academics.

As we have seen above the leading advocates of 'thoughtful' strategic management argue that sustainable decisions can only be achieved in the context of a dialectical framework within which strategic planning and strategic thinking work in tandem. In most areas of political and commercial life, plans are constantly altered to meet changed technological, social, economic, political, or legal circumstances. Many (possibly most) strategic reviews are overtly pragmatic in nature and are triggered by changing circumstances. They represent reactive responses to actual or anticipated changes in external conditions. It might be argued that this form of change management, although legitimate, does not qualify as 'strategic thinking' of the kind we are here proposing. This is because it fails to embrace creative reflection, is overly reactive, and sees the future as a modified projection of the present rather than as a newly conceived 'better' place.

Henry Mintzberg (1994) has been influential in arguing that strategic thinking is not merely "an alternative nomenclature for everything falling under the umbrella of strategic management": it is, he argues, a particular way of thinking with specific and clearly discernible characteristics. In explaining the difference between strategic planning and strategic thinking, Mintzberg argues that strategic planning involves the systematic programming of pre-determined strategies from which action plans (corporate, financial, departmental and individual) are developed. Strategic thinking, on the other hand, is a synthesizing process utilising intuition and creativity that produces an integrated perspective of the enterprise. The strategically thoughtful organisation operates with added coherence because its strategic planning takes place within a framework of thought-out shared understandings of its purpose and potential. There are, of course, a number of psychological and organisational barriers to the establishment of this kind of shared thoughtfulness and it is these that constitute the subject matter of this book.

The notion of 'strategic thinking' in the sense we are using here, should not simply be regarded as "thinking about strategy": to do so leads to confusion and fails to make the requisite distinction between thinking and planning. Mintzberg does not see the notion as a deeper or improved version of strategic planning and summarises his understanding of the concept by emphasising that in contrast to planning, strategic thinking in its purest form, places a strong emphasis on the general themes of creativity, exploration, and understanding corporate discontinuities. In rationality analysis we tend to reconceive 'discontinuities' as 'multiple rationalities'. In this way, the key issue is not so much seen as 'filling gaps' as 'reconciling multiple points of view'.

As a way of getting some sort of intellectual purchase on the idea (and following Mintzberg's general thesis), both Jeanne Liedtka and Eton Lawrence suggest that strategic thinking might be considered as embracing five key perspectives. In considering this model we need to bear in mind – indeed understand – that the nature and scope of each of Liedtka's elements is open to interpretation and what is being sought is an inter-subjective agreement about how they are constituted.

Liedtka postulates that strategic thinking can be treated as comprising five key elements (see fig.2).

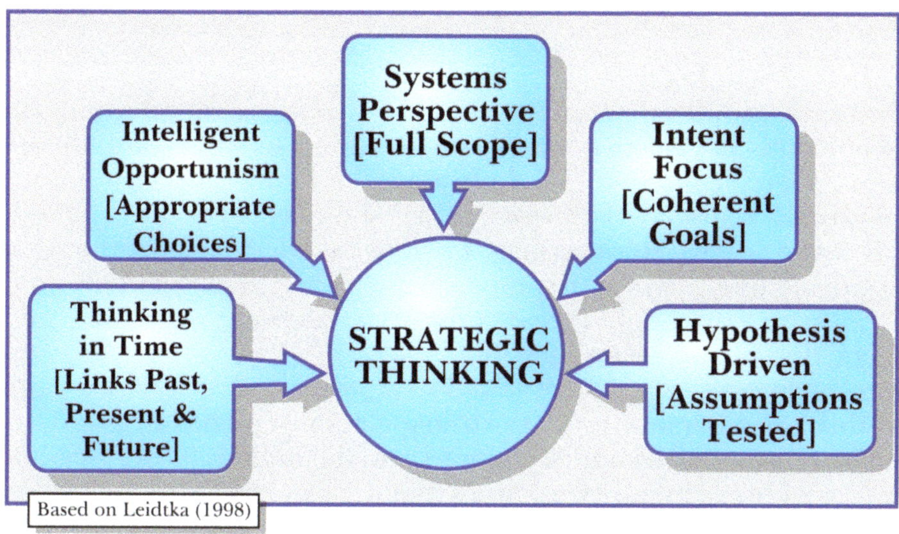

Figure 2: Elements of Strategic Thinking

1. Systems perspective

This considers the scope of the various business activities and focuses on the their internal and external connections. It suggests that strategic thinkers make a point of setting discussions about an organisation's strategy into the context of the overall system of value creation of which it is a part. This involves appreciating that many business problems result from some form of 'systems failure' (Senge 1990) that in turn results from a lack of proper understanding of the inter-connected nature of business activity.

> *"The systems perspective enables individuals to clarify their role within the larger system and the impact of their behaviour on other parts of the system, as well as on the final outcome. This approach addresses, therefore, not only the fit between the corporate, business, and functional levels of strategy, but very importantly, the person level." (Lawrence 1999)*

A systems perspective enables actors not only to acquire a reflective view of their role within the organisation, but also to appreciate both how all the horizontal linkages within the organisation interconnect and how the organisation and its departments engage vertically with the external world and its associated social and economic arrangements. In this sense the systems thinker is consciously 'non-parochial' and is aware of the wider consequences of his/her own and other people's actions.

2. Intent-focused

In contrast to the systems perspective that focuses on questions of 'scope', this perspective focuses on questions of 'time' and 'direction'. Strategic intent highlights the need for coherent decisions to be grounded in shared understandings about what is to be achieved when and where. Some writers, Liedtka included, suggest that the notion of 'intent' has a psychological aspect and ideally its adoption should convey not only a sense of direction but also a sense of excitement, discovery or even "destiny".

In this way, an intent focus to strategic management can not only set targets that bring added coherence to the organisation's goals, it can provide a framework of values that can establish a clear identity for the corporate team that helps them and others to appreciate the organization's market (or other operating area) and its place in the wider community. It can also energise those within the organization to play an effective part in achieving the corporate goals. In this way, it can be regarded as an underlying component of the business culture and, among other things, can have positive impacts on organizational effectiveness as well as staff recruitment and retention. To use a couple of metaphors taken from orienteering, we might say that by establishing a coherent and shared understanding of the organisation's mission, we create a compass that will make it easier to 'weather the storms' of change and to 'stay on course' when business conditions become challenging.

Clearly, the idea of 'strategic intent' is directly related to, and dependent upon, the pre-existence of a 'systems focus'. Just as obviously, for intentionality to have any real effect, it has to be shared and understood by all participants (at all levels) within the organisation. So, at this point we can assert that truly effective strategic management has to involve more than boards of management and those with an executive function (see below sections 'intelligent opportunism' and 'barriers to strategic thinking').
The business culture and its functional systems need to accommo-

date the fact that in virtually every field of commercial, voluntary and political activity, adaptation to change is a continuing need. It is inevitable that the organisation will constantly need to rethink and reshape its 'intent focus'.

3. Intelligent opportunism

This element focuses on 'openness' and 'imagination'. In response to the ever-changing nature of social, economic and political systems (relating to societal attitudes, markets, laws and regulations), corporate strategies need to be subjected to constant review. The issue here is about how to make the most appropriate choice of strategic change and development.

It is generally held that in practising intelligent opportunism, it is important that organisations encourage inputs from lower level employees or more innovative staff whose knowledge and experience could be instrumental in identifying particular strategies that might otherwise be missed. For example, according to Lawrence, Intel's dominant role in the microprocessor industry was largely the result of non-executive technical staff acting in defiance of senior management's stated strategic objectives. Many firms utilise the fresh (yet-to-be institutionalised) impressions of new appointees to critique aspects of their current ideas and practices. In a similar way, some make a point of inviting those retiring or moving to new jobs to use their experiences of working for the organization to comment on aspects of its policy or practices.

Some analysts (e.g. Hamel and Prahalad 1997) argue that 'head office' executives tend to work within a form of senior management culture that inhibits certain types imagination and that there is a tendency for creative thinking (particularly about technical issues and customer relations) to occur more readily 'downstream' away from the CEO's desk. It is also in these less influential locations that we find new and younger employees whose thinking is often less institutionalised than that of their older and more established colleagues. If asked, such members of staff are likely to proffer more laterally orientated thoughts about strategic change and development and, for the 'thinking organisation', failure to capture these ideas is not seen simply as a failure to be inclusive but, more significantly, as a lost opportunity or even as a corporate risk. All of this leads to the conclusion that effective strategic management requires the organization to incorporate a commitment to a culture of communication that actively encourages all staff to interact around ideas and yet-to-be- considered possibilities.

4. Thinking in time

According to Hamel and Prahalad (1994), strategy is not solely driven by a shared understanding of the changing nature of future systems, but also by an appreciation of the gap between the current reality and the organisation's emerging intent for the future. In other words, when the external business environment changes, the organisation becomes motivated to respond reactively – but in the thinking organisation, the opportunity is taken at this time to reconsider its goals and intentions in a creative and proactive way. From a socio-economic perspective, the overriding strategic intention of the thinking firm would be continually to adjust its employment of limited resources to produce 'best value' outcomes .[144]

Every organisation has a history that has created experiential knowledge and obligations. It has a present that has to be 'lived' in the moment (displaying a range of current practices and problems that have to be managed now). It has a future that will impose both external changes and create new corporate aspirations. Whereas the traditional view of strategy focuses on the degree of fit between existing resources and current opportunities, a strategic intent approach considers a more fundamental lack of fit between resources and ambitions. Thus, by connecting the past with the present and linking this to the future, strategic thinking is always "thinking in time."

> *"Strategic thinking connects the past, present, and future and in this way uses both an institution's memory and its broad historical context as critical inputs into the creation of its future. This oscillation between the past, present, and future is essential for both strategy formulation and execution." (Lawrence).*

Charles Handy (1994) underlines the importance of thinking in time by making the point that effective strategic plans not only have

[144] The notion of 'best value' was developed by social and welfare economists in the 1990s. It seeks to provide a 'socially responsive' take on the question of what constitutes value-for-money: refer Garnett D (2015) pp. 202-8.

to be responsive to change, but coherent and stable. They need both a sense of continuity with the past and a sense of direction for the future so that in the present they can maintain a feeling of control in the midst of change. From this perspective, the real question is not what does the future we are trying to create look like, rather it is: 'having envisioned the future that we agree we want to create, what must we keep from that past, lose from the past, and create in the present, to get there?'

5. Hypothesis-Driven

A hypothesis is a supposition or proposed explanation made on the basis of limited evidence. In essence it is a provisional explanation of a state of affairs and in science it represents a starting point for further investigation. It is an explanation that is yet to be verified and it is assumed that further investigation will help reinforce, modify or disprove its veracity. In philosophy a hypothesis is more of a 'conjecture' and represents a reasoned proposition made as a basis for further thought, without any assumption of its truth.

The employment of hypotheses is regarded to be an essential aspect not only of the scientific method, but also of strategic thinking. This is because of the recognition that, to some degree, creativity requires the thinking strategist to utilise intuition and imagination as well as analytical reasoning. To use a modern turn of phrase derived from American baseball slang, we might say that some great ideas come "out of left field". This means that creative strategic thinking requires the reconciliation of intuition and critical judgement. Hypothesis testing is used to overcome the potential dichotomy that can exist between intuitive and analytical thought.[145]

The argument is that hypothesis-testing enables imagination to operate in conjunction with analysis through a sequentially structured discursive process of iteration that generates, tests and continually refines assumptions about right action. Arguably, the biggest issue with hypothesis-testing is that people try and prove that their current (favourite) hypothesis is correct by selecting examples of evidence that confirm it and ignore those that that would challenge or undermine it.

[145] See chapter 6 for fuller discussion of this idea.

Derived from the scientific method but operated in the context of political administration and business management, the adoption of hypothesis-driven thinking implies that the organisation embraces a culture of research and learning. It also implies that managers and executive leaders are prepared to engage in speculative thought (sometimes referred to as "What If" speculations). Leidtka comments that in her experience, not all CEOs and senior managers are comfortable working in such a culture. The same hesitancy can be detected amongst central and local government leaders. This may be because some of those in authority dislike the level of uncertainty that is implicit in such an approach or because discursive management costs time and money for which the returns are not immediately apparent. It may also be true that some committees and management boards signal a degree of concern (or even disquiet) when their executive managers indicate that strategic policies are being 'researched' rather than 'enacted'. To a certain type of business mind, certainty brings clarity and comfort - but, as Tony Schwartz has famously pointed out,[146] the opposite of certainty is not uncertainty, but openness, curiosity and a willingness to embrace paradox – in short, those factors that are the essence of multiple rationality analysis. It is clearly true that if strategic thinking is to have operational relevance it must at some point be operationalized through a process of convergent and systematic analysis. If it is to be more than an isolated act of self-indulgence, strategic thinking has to engage with the processes of strategic planning.

Barriers to strategic thinking

A research orientated thinking/learning culture can only flourish if it is welcomed and encouraged by those in senior management positions. Ironically, 'bottom-up' influence can only prosper where 'top-down' authority allows it. The academic literature captures the notion of 'reflection in action' to describe a situation in which practitioners work in ways that accommodate innovative thinking throughout the organization. This notion reflects the point that, although particular events may trigger new ideas, sometimes desirable change occurs as a result of practitioners reflecting on what they do and how they do it. The full positive effects of such

[146] In 'Turning 60: The twelve most important lessons I've learned so far'. Much quoted in the management literature. https://hbr.org/2012/05/turning-60-the-twelve-most.html

reflection can only be harnessed in those organisations where the over-arching strategic intent of the business is known and understood by all employees.

We have already suggested that for some executives, this open approach to management thinking can be felt to be disturbing or even dangerous. It is not simply concerns about the necessary time and other resource commitments that can lead to managerial anxieties about this approach - deep-seated worries can also exist that once people start to reflect-in-action, unthought-of operational complexities will surface and these will bring confusion to what is currently clear. "We're running smoothly, but if we think too much about what we're doing, it might lead to operational paralysis." The fear here is that "too much" reflection-in-action will trigger a never-ending cycle of complexity. In short, there can be an instinctive feeling amongst some managers and politicians that thinking and doing are not, as we are arguing here, necessary. Indeed for some, they are not even seen to be compatible. Where such a diffident (or even antagonistic) attitude prevails, it is unlikely that senior staff will be motivated to (or even see the point of) shifting the corporate culture towards open thinking. In such cases the approach to strategic management is likely to remain impoverished, and will remain so, until the organisation operates under new leadership.

BIBLIOGRAPHY TO APPENDIX

'Hambrick and Fredrickson (2001) 'Are you sure you have a strategy?' *In the Academy of Management Executive* (2001), Vol.15., No.4.

Heracleous, L. (1998). Strategic thinking or strategic planning, *Long Range Planning, 31*, (3), 481-487.

Lawrence E. (1999) *Strategic Thinking : A Discussion Paper,* Public Services Commission of Canada.

Liedtka, J. (1998). *Strategic thinking; can it be taught?, Long Range Planning, 31*, (1), 120-129.

Liedtka, J. (1998). Linking strategic thinking with strategic planning, *Strategy and Leadership, October*, (1), 120-129.

Mintzberg H. (1994), *The Rise and Fall of Strategic Planning*, Basic Books.

Porter M, 'What is Strategy?' (1996) *Harvard Business Review (Nov-Dec).*

The Blind Men and The Elephant.

A Hindoo Fable.

I. It was six men of Indostan
To learning much inclined,
Who went to see the Elephant
(Though all of them were blind),
That each by observation
Might satisfy his mind.

II. The First approached the Elephant,
And happening to fall
Against his broad and sturdy side,
At once began to bawl:
"God bless me!—but the Elephant
Is very like a wall!"

III. The Second, feeling of the tusk,
Cried: "Ho!—what have we here
So very round and smooth and sharp?
To me 'tis mighty clear
This wonder of an Elephant
Is very like a spear!"

IV. The Third approached the animal,
And happening to take
The squirming trunk within his hands,
Thus boldly up and spake:
"I see," quoth he, "the Elephant
Is very like a snake!"

V. The Fourth reached out his eager hand,
And felt about the knee.
"What most this wondrous beast is like
Is mighty plain," quoth he;
" 'tis clear enough the Elephant
Is very like a tree!"

VI. The Fifth, who chanced to touch the ear,
Said: "E'en the blindest man
Can tell what this resembles most;
Deny the fact who can,
This marvel of an Elephant
Is very like a fan!"

VII. The Sixth no sooner had begun
About the beast to grope,
Than, seizing on the swinging tail
That fell within his scope,
"I see," quoth he, "the Elephant
Is very like a rope!"

VIII. And so these men of Indostan
Disputed loud and long,
Each in his own opinion
Exceeding stiff and strong,
Though each was partly in the right,
And all were in the wrong!

MORAL.
So, oft in theologic wars
The disputants, I ween,
Rail on in utter ignorance
Of what each other mean,
And prate about an Elephant
Not one of them has seen!

INDEX

Index

N

P

R

S

T

U

V

W

Lightning Source UK Ltd.
Milton Keynes UK
UKHW020607010520
362619UK00002B/15